To Paul
We lived this great
adventure — I hope
you enjoy this remarkable
rescue too.
Best wishes Christmas 1996
Stewie.

Rescue in the Southern Ocean

Penguin Books Australia Ltd
487 Maroondah Highway, PO Box 257
Ringwood, Victoria 3134, Australia
Penguin Books Ltd
Harmondsworth, Middlesex, England
Viking Penguin, A Division of
Penguin Books USA Inc.
375 Hudson Street, New York
New York 10014, USA
Penguin Books Canada Limited
10 Alcorn Avenue, Toronto, Ontario
Canada M4V 3B2
Penguin Books (NZ) Ltd
Cnr Rosedale and Airborne Roads, Albany
Auckland, New Zealand

First published by Penguin Books
Australia Ltd, 1997
in association with *The Age*, Melbourne

10 9 8 7 6 5 4 3 2 1

Typeset in 9.5/13 Stone Serif
Made and printed in Australia by
Southbank Book, Melbourne

National Library of Australia
Cataloguing-in-Publication data:

Rescue in the Southern Ocean

ISBN 0 14 026837 5.

1. Dubois, Thierry. 2. Dinelli, Raphael.
3. Bullimore, Tony. 4. Australian Defence
Force – Search and rescue operations.
5. Search and rescue operations – Antarctic
Ocean. 6. Rescues – Antarctic Ocean.
7. Survival after airplane accidents,
shipwrecks, etc. 8. Marine accidents –
Antarctic Ocean.

363.148109167

RESCUE
IN THE SOUTHERN OCEAN

Penguin Books
in association with *The Age*, Melbourne

Thousands of kilometres out to sea, the oceans and the winds dictate the rules – and the sailors know it.

Vendee Globe – the Solo Sailor's Mount Everest

Likened to the Mount Everest of yacht racing, the Vendee Globe solo round-the-world yacht race has the reputation as the toughest and most dangerous single-handed challenge on water. Enthusiasts claim it is the most searching test of humankind and machine, on water or on land.

The race was originally conceived by Phillipe Jeantot, who established himself in the 1980s as one of the world's finest single-handed ocean racers and is now the race director. 'The Vendee Globe was created to answer the needs of sailors eager to reach their uppermost limits,' he said.

The Vendee Globe follows in the spirit of the Golden Globe of 1968, the first unassisted solo race. Briton Robin Knox-Johnston was the winner – and the only finisher to obey all the rules. The Vendee Globe has roots in the BOC round-the-world solo four-stage race from the eastern United States, run periodically since 1983, and won twice by Jeantot.

The race starts from Les Sables d'Olonne on the French Atlantic coast in the Vendee region. The course takes competitors south across the Bay of Biscay and along the African coast towards the Cape of Good Hope, gateway to the notoriously treacherous Southern Ocean. The race passes three capes – the Cape of Good Hope, Cape Leeuwin and Cape Horn.

Two-thirds of the race traverse the huge seas, limitless grey skies and shrieking gales of the Southern Ocean. Historically, this vast expanse has instilled fear into sailors on vessels much bigger than those in the Vendee Globe. It is one of the most desolate regions on earth, where competitors race through the Roaring Forties and the Furious Fifties. Few ships pass through here; land is thousands of miles away; it is cold, friendless and the weather never relaxes. It is the Southern Ocean south-west of Australia that has proved to be most difficult. According to the CSIRO, these waters have the strongest winds and some of the largest waves in the world.

The rules entail an unassisted, non-stop, single-handed race. In the previous two Vendee races, only half the competitors finished within the rules; such is the prestige of the race that skippers disqualified by seeking aid often continue unofficially. Entrants must have completed an authenticated single-handed transoceanic voyage of not less than 10 000 miles using a mono-hull of 15.2 to 18.3 metres. Rules also demand a series of safety measures on each yacht but say: 'The crew has no right to expect the organising committee of the race to set up rescue operations from land.'

For many onlookers around the world the Vendee Globe is better known for the death and tragedy it has brought than for any celebration of human effort. In the 1989–90 race, only seven of the thirteen starters finished. One week into the second race, in 1992–93, Nigel Burgess of Monaco disappeared in the Atlantic in circumstances still unexplained. In the same race Isabelle Autissier had to be rescued south of Australia. Of the 14 starters, six finished.

The race is dominated by French sailors, who have established a respected reputation for long-distance solo racing, not only by Jeantot, but by others such as the multi-hull sailor Alain Colas, and previous Vendee winners Titouan Lamazou and Alain Gaultier. Lamazou set the record of 109 days in 1990.

Despite the experience of these sailors, in the Vendee Globe they face conditions they previously only heard about and are likely to come closer to death than at any other time in the years they have spent on water. They face giant waves that toss their yachts about like corks. Cascading walls of water surround their boats. Waves crash onto decks with such ferocity that equipment and rigging are ripped to pieces, forcing the sailors to spend days below deck for safety.

The 1996–97 Vendee Globe was marked by the dramatic rescues of Raphael Dinelli, Thierry Dubois and Tony Bullimore, among the greatest sea dramas ever witnessed in peacetime. This account captures the epic story of their rescues in words and pictures, filed as the events unfolded.

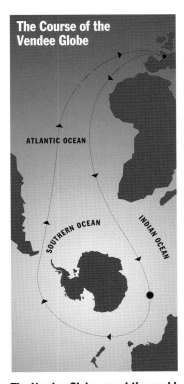

The Vendee Globe round-the-world yacht race has been labelled by 'Seahorse Sailing', the official magazine of the Royal Ocean Racing Club, as 'the purist's marathon . . . one event (which) stands head and shoulders above all others in terms of the outright personal challenge it presents'.

The Course of the Vendee Globe

Beginning and ending at the port of Les Sables d'Olonne on the French Atlantic coast, the Vendee Globe takes competitors around three capes — the Cape of Good Hope, Cape Leeuwin and Cape Horn. Two-thirds of the race traverse the notoriously treacherous Southern Ocean.

Les Sables d'Olonne

Cape of Good Hope

Cape Leeuwin

The Lure of the Sea

Thierry Dubois

French-born Dubois, 29, sailed solo in the Southern Ocean for the first time during the 1996–97 Vendee Globe on his 1989 yacht, *Pour Amnesty International*. He won the 1993 Mini-Transat Race and finished second in the 1995 Round Europe Race.

'I have to win this race. This is the most famous race. I don't know anything better than this.'

Raphael Dinelli

Dinelli, 28, was born in France and has been sailing since he was sixteen. He was granted unofficial entrant status in the 1996–97 Vendee Globe and was the youngest competitor in the field. His boat, *Algimouss*, was launched in 1988, and had already been raced twice around the world by Vendee Globe race organiser Phillipe Jeantot.

'My life is the sea, and I love the race.'

'Of the few things left on this Earth that I want to do, the Vendee Globe represents the major race, the major challenge. So I will do it.'

Tony Bullimore

English-born Tony Bullimore, 58, has competed in some of the world's most gruelling races and is regarded as one of Britain's most experienced sailors. He sailed the 20-metre ketch, *Global Exide Challenger* in the 1996–97 Vendee Globe, a yacht that he built and designed in 1992 of carbon-kelvar.

He has won many races since his first Atlantic race in 1976. In 1985 he was voted joint Yachtsman of the Year with his sailing partner, Nigel Irens, by the Yachting Journalists' Association after winning the Round Britain Race, the Round the Island Race off the Isle of Wight and the Round Britain and Ireland Race. He also won his class in the Round Europe Race. During a 1976 solo trans-Atlantic race, he was rescued from his life raft by an oil tanker after his trimaran burst into flames. In 1989 he was skippering a yacht that flipped over during trials, killing one of the crew. He has been described as aggressive, strong, kind, generous and does not fear adversity. Tony Bullimore's wife of 35 years, Lalel, knows her husband best, and her characterisation of him is perhaps the most accurate: 'sea dog'.

25 December 1996

• Raphael Dinelli's yacht, *Algimouss*, rolls over 1200 nautical miles south of Australia.

• Dinelli scrambles free and climbs onto the near-submerged hull of his upturned yacht. He sets off a hand-held distress beacon that is heard in France. His 30-hour wait begins.

26 December 1996

8.51 p.m. (EST)
• P-3C Orion, Rescue 251, locates Dinelli's yacht and drops emergency supplies and two inflatable life rafts. With minutes to spare Dinelli scrambles aboard the raft.

27 December 1996

• Peter Goss turns his yacht *Aqua Quorum* to rescue Dinelli. He is guided to Dinelli by an RAAF Orion crew, Rescue 251 and 252.

11.30 a.m.
• Dinelli picked up by Goss.

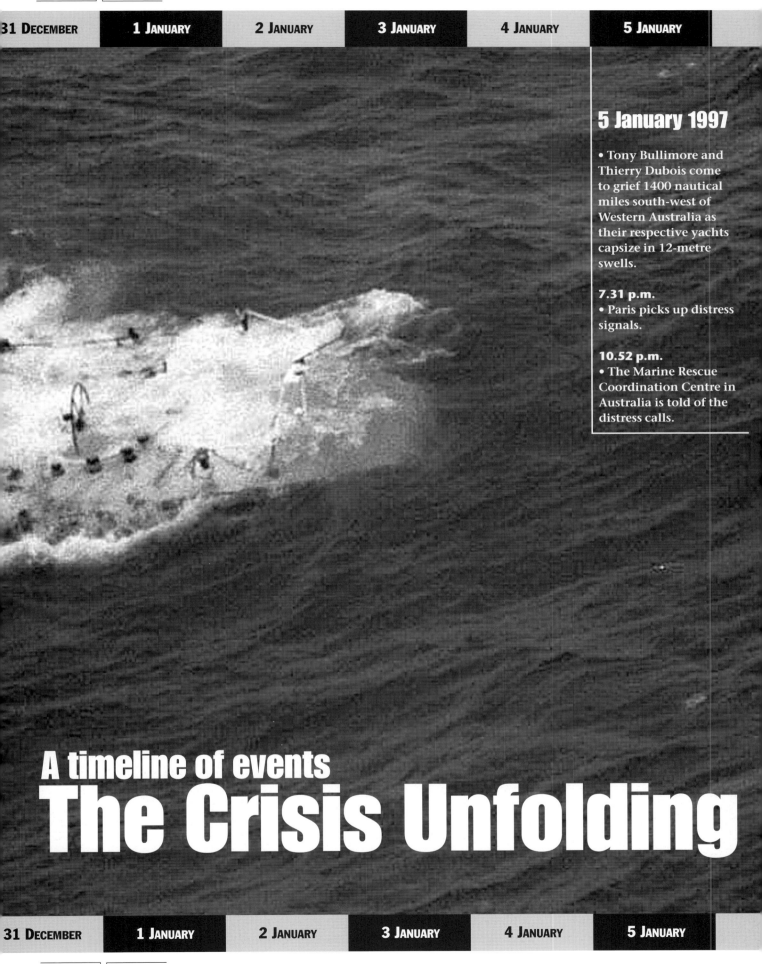

5 January 1997

• Tony Bullimore and Thierry Dubois come to grief 1400 nautical miles south-west of Western Australia as their respective yachts capsize in 12-metre swells.

7.31 p.m.
• Paris picks up distress signals.

10.52 p.m.
• The Marine Rescue Coordination Centre in Australia is told of the distress calls.

A timeline of events
The Crisis Unfolding

6 January 1997

12.51 a.m.
• Emergency Services pick up four ARGOS beacons from two yachts in the area.
• RAAF Edinburgh is told that P-3C Orion aircraft from 92 Wing will be required for the search.

1.20 a.m.
• Request of military assistance passed to Headquarters Australian Defence Force (HQADF).

2.09 a.m.
• Further ARGOS positions received.

2.10 a.m.
• Search-planning in progress. Marine Rescue Coordination Centre in contact with the French mission control centre, Emergency Services, Airservices Australia and the Australian Defence Force to effect the rescue of the distressed craft.

3.33 a.m.
• *Sanko Phoenix*, the nearest merchant ship 56 hours away, is advised to proceed to the distress position to assist.

11.21 a.m.
• RAAF P-3C Orion refuels in Perth and heads for the search area.
• Reports of winds of over 100 kmh and ten-metre swells. Air temperature is 1° C and water about 5° C.

4.05 p.m.
• The upturned hull of *Pour Amnesty International* is sighted by RAAF P-3C Orion, Rescue 251. Dubois is sighted clinging to the keel.

4.50 p.m.
• RAAF P-3C Orion, Rescue 251, drops Dubois an air sea rescue kit containing two self-inflating rafts.

5.00 p.m.
• 92 Wing launches another two Orions from RAAF Edinburgh to assist in the rescue.

7.00 p.m.
• HMAS *Adelaide* departs Western Australia.

9.30 p.m.
• Dubois settles in life raft dropped by Rescue 252.

9.50 p.m.
• RAAF P-3C Orion, Rescue 252, sights the upturned hull of *Global Exide Challenger* without its keel. There is no sign of Bullimore.
• A new signal that can only be switched on manually is picked up from the yacht.

10.00 p.m.
• Fifth Orion crew deployed to Perth on board a RAAF Hercules.

10.35 p.m.
• Further ARGOS positions received.

7 January 1997

9.15 a.m.
• Details of hull compartments for *Global Exide Challenger* are passed on to HMAS *Adelaide*.

11.00 a.m.
• RAAF P-3C Orions continue to fly over the distress craft and beacon detection positions.

1.15 p.m.
• Situation updates with HMAS *Adelaide* and *Sanko Phoenix*.

3.00 p.m.
• Assessments are made of possibilities for entering the hull of the *Global Exide Challenger*.

4.45 p.m.
• Successful helibox drop with radio to Dubois in life raft from RAAF P-3C Orion, Rescue 253.

5.30 p.m.
• Radio communication established between RAAF P-3C Orion, Rescue 253, and Dubois.
• Establish that Dubois's distress was due to three successive capsizes and advises that he has enough food and water to last for three days.

9.45 p.m.
• Search continues for Bullimore. RAAF P-3C Orion, Rescue 254, reports some rope and a pink buoy observed in the search area.

8 January 1997

1.15 a.m.
• Information from the boat builder and Emergency Services beacon positioning on *Global Exide Challenger* indicate that Bullimore could still be alive and inside the inverted boat.

3.00 a.m.
• Plans are made to drop sonobuoys and electronic underwater noise makers close to *Global Exide Challenger* to listen for possible signs of life.

9.50 a.m.
• Sonobuoys and electronic noise makers are dropped by Rescue 256 and subsequent Orion aircraft.

1.45 p.m.
• RAAF P-3C Orion, Rescue 257, reports very bad weather in the projected rescue area.

2.30 p.m.
• HMAS *Adelaide* defers winching decision due to bad weather: low level air temperature reported –2˚ C.

3.00 p.m.
• Full technical plans in place for penetrating the hull of *Global Exide Challenger*.

10.00 p.m.
• HMAS *Westralia* departs HMAS Sterling, near Perth, to refuel HMAS *Adelaide*.

9 January 1997

2.30 a.m.
• Regular tapping sounds picked up from the hull of Bullimore's yacht by RAAF P-3C Orion, Rescue 259, some 30 minutes after electronic noise maker is activated.

7.00 a.m.
• RAAF P-3C Orion, Rescue 260, monitors rescue of Dubois by RAN Seahawk helicopter and guides HMAS *Adelaide* to the position of the *Global Exide Challenger*.

7.15 a.m.
• Dubois rescued and evacuated from the life raft by a helicopter from HMAS *Adelaide*.
• HMAS *Adelaide* now proceeding to *Global Exide Challenger*.

11.45 a.m.
• HMAS *Adelaide* reports that it has picked up Bullimore.
• Earlier, they had sent out a Rigid Inflatable Boat (RIB) to the *Global Exide Challenger* with a crew of engineers and divers. Bullimore swam out from under the hull – he had been in an air-locked cabin beneath the submerged yacht.
•The distress call is cancelled.

3.00 p.m.
• Bullimore receives medical treatment aboard HMAS *Adelaide*.

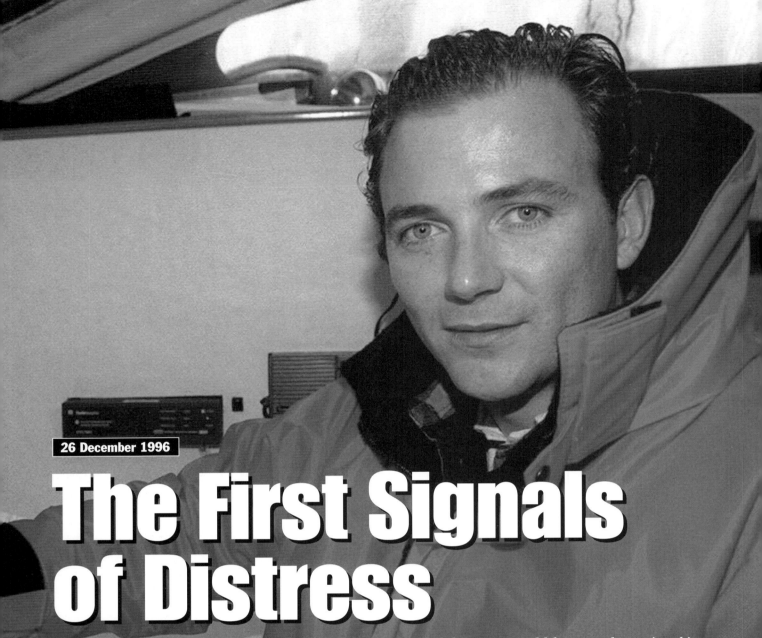

26 December 1996

The First Signals of Distress

Raphael Dinelli

Raphael Dinelli activated three emergency beacons early on Boxing Day. It was not known whether he was disabled or in distress because there was no voice contact.

On Christmas Day he reported to France 'terrible wind gusts' of up to 60 to 70 knots after passing the Kergulen Islands, halfway between Cape Town and Perth. He also reported interior damage to his 18-metre sloop, *Algimouss*, after it was twice laid on its side. 'All is in disorder but the mast is always there,' he said. 'It is not a lot of fun.'

RAAF Orion, call sign Rescue 251, flew out of Perth to seek Dinelli's yacht in latitude 53 degrees south, an area of open ocean known for its continuous cold fronts and occasional icebergs. But locating the yachtsman was difficult because of the appalling weather conditions and the short duration of the signals from the beacon. The Orion had to rely on coordinates supplied from France.

At 8.51 p.m., after a six-hour search, Dinelli's yacht was located by Rescue 251. He was alive.

Despite strong winds, poor visibility, low cloud and a 3.5-metre swell, the Orion dropped emergency supplies and two inflatable life rafts to Dinelli. The plane then returned to Perth. With minutes to spare Dinelli scrambled upon the life raft dropped by RAAF P-3C Orion, Rescue 251. Ten minutes later *Algimouss* sank beneath the water's surface.

AUSTRALIA

Rescued yachtsman Raphael Dinelli

50°

Southern Ocean

ANTARCTICA

The rescue area, 2200 km south-west of Perth.

Miles from nowhere, a lone sailor gets a lifeline

Raphael Dinelli knee-deep in water on his submerged vessel.

Dinelli prepares his life raft for rescue shortly before being picked up by a rival yachtsman in the Vendee Globe race, Peter Goss. Dinelli's yacht, Algimouss, sank just ten minutes after he reached the life raft.

'He has just been saved from almost certain death.'

27 December 1996

After 36 hours of misery at sea – at times standing knee-deep in icy water on his submerged yacht – Christmas finally arrived for Raphael Dinelli in the shape of fellow sailing competitor, Peter Goss. Goss, 35, a former Royal Marine, hauled Dinelli, who was suffering hypothermia and bruises, onto his yacht *Aqua Quorum* about 2200 kilometres south-west of Perth.

Goss, who put aside his dreams of victory in the Vendee Globe race to sail to the rescue of his stricken friend, said that picking up Dinelli was 'the best Christmas present' he's ever had.

Goss was guided to the stricken 18-metre sloop by two RAAF Orions, Rescue 251 and Rescue 252, which spotted Dinelli on 26 December.

'He has just been saved from almost certain death,' said the tactical coordinator of Rescue 252, Flight Lieutenant Garrick Richards.

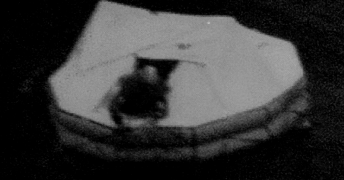

Peter Goss took 15 hours to travel 65 nautical miles through wild seas to his stricken colleague. He nursed Dinelli through the 11-day voyage that finished in Hobart. 'Raphael's story is incredible,' Goss told organisers. 'He was close to death on several occasions, but each time something happened to save him.

'For example, he had lost his life raft when the aircraft dropped him a new one. He is an exceptional sailor who kept a cool head under enormous pressure. He has made his own good fortune and it is my privilege to have him on board.'

Welcome aboard! Dinelli is hauled to safety by Goss off Western Australia.

Peter Goss sails to Raphael Dinelli's rescue in his yacht, Aqua Quorum.

Two hands join across the waves

Peter Goss in Hobart in the early hours of 8 January aboard Aqua Quorum.

'We know that we would one day regret what we have left behind, but this is the sea and this is the lure.'

It was one of life's odder friendships, British yachting lifesaver Peter Goss mused. 'It's funny, isn't it? You do a single-handed race and make friends in the Southern Ocean.' He knew Raphael Dinelli only from a single handshake and a few words – 'Take care, have a good race and be safe' – exchanged before the start of the race in November.

Dinelli didn't expect Goss as his rescuer. He thought the conditions were too bad for the Briton to come back to him, and he would have to rely on a Frenchman sailing behind. Frozen stiff with cold, Dinelli was put in the sole bunk aboard *Aqua Quorum* by Goss, who had to steer despite his fatigue. He nursed the Frenchman with radioed medical advice. After about four days, Dinelli recovered enough to move about.

'He needed to talk a lot. You get on a survivor's high. In fact you couldn't stop him bloody talking.' Most absorbing for them were the

challenges of yacht racing and, particularly, the safety of sailors. Both men talked about the Southern Ocean's 'black spot' south-west of Australia; why it took such a toll on racing yachts, and tried to come up with some answers. While sitting in the RAAF life raft, Dinelli had mentally redesigned all life rafts.

It was a strange parting when the time came. Dinelli dropped a lunchtime pizza off to his 'rescue man' before heading out to Hobart airport, saying to Goss, 'my heart is with your heart.' Dinelli vowed to keep in touch with Goss every step of the way. 'It is very important for him and me to stay in communication,' Dinelli said, 'because this is my rescue man.'

Goss and Dinelli both believe that they – and all Vendee Globe sailors – are fighters. They, and others like them, will make sacrifices and endure hardships to pursue their passion; they will not give up. 'We know that we would one day regret what we have left behind,' Dinelli said, 'but this is the sea and this is the lure.'

Dinelli vows to sail again

Top: Raphael Dinelli (left) and Peter Goss on arrival in Hobart, Tasmania.
Bottom: The joy of rescue.

Despite almost drowning, and suffering frostbite and hypothermia, rescued yachtsman Raphael Dinelli declared that he would continue sailing. 'I love sailing now and I need to (be) sailing because it's my life.'

He said he thought he would die in the Southern Ocean after his yacht *Algimouss* capsized in near-freezing waters about 2200 km south-west of Perth on Christmas Day. 'When I heard the plane, it was a miracle for me,' he said.

Asked what he wanted to say to the Australian rescue authorities, Dinelli replied: 'Merci beaucoup, thanks a lot. This is a happy Christmas . . . a happy present for me.'

Left: Raphael Dinelli arrives in Melbourne from Hobart: 'A good wind . . . not too strong,' he said. 'A good wind for the sailing.'

Further drama south of the 50th parallel

More Signals of Distress

Two more distress calls were received late on Sunday, 5 January, from French competitor Thierry Dubois, 29, on *Pour Amnesty International*, and Briton Tony Bullimore, 58, on *Global Exide Challenger*.

The frigate HMAS *Adelaide* was pressed into service but would not reach the stricken yachts, about 1400 nautical miles south-west of Perth, for two and a half days.

RAAF P-3C Orion, Rescue 251, departed from RAAF Edinburgh and stopped for refuelling in Perth at 11.44 a.m. on 6 January, before continuing on to the yachtsmen.

The rescue operation is further from shore than any previous rescue. The second Orion, Rescue 252, departs Perth at 4.44 p.m. With no yachts within 1000 nautical miles, and no merchant ships within five days' sailing, the flights are the yachtmen's last hope.

The last hope for Dubois and Bullimore: the RAAF P-3C Orion.

To the rescue

The Air-Sea Rescue Kit

How it is dropped: ASRK is a chain of four packages connected by rope. It is dropped upwind of the stricken vessel in the hope that the rope falls across it. The outer two packages are life rafts and the other two contain emergency supplies.

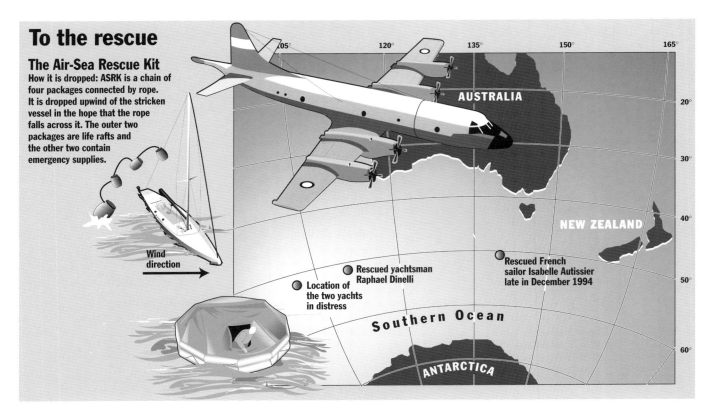

Wind direction

Location of the two yachts in distress

Rescued yachtsman Raphael Dinelli

Rescued French sailor Isabelle Autissier late in December 1994

AUSTRALIA

NEW ZEALAND

Southern Ocean

ANTARCTICA

The race to get Dubois

The HMAS Adelaide is expected to be within 100 nautical miles by 7.30 am. A Seahawk helicopter will then cover the remaining distance to reach Dubois within an expected 90 minutes flying time.

Once the helicopter is over the sailor, a navy crewman will be lowered to the life raft to lift the by now exhausted Dubois back to the helicopter, which will then return to HMAS Adelaide.

Once Dubois has been safely brought back to the ship, the search will then continue for the other missing yachtsman Tony Bullimore, whose boat is thought to be about 55 nautical miles away. Rescuers are hoping to find him within the hull of his upturned yacht.

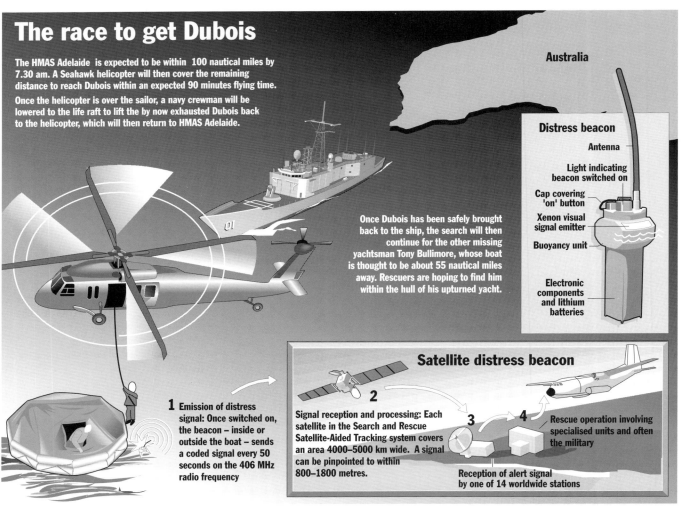

Australia

Distress beacon

Antenna

Light indicating beacon switched on

Cap covering 'on' button

Xenon visual signal emitter

Buoyancy unit

Electronic components and lithium batteries

1 Emission of distress signal: Once switched on, the beacon – inside or outside the boat – sends a coded signal every 50 seconds on the 406 MHz radio frequency

Satellite distress beacon

2 Signal reception and processing: Each satellite in the Search and Rescue Satellite-Aided Tracking system covers an area 4000–5000 km wide. A signal can be pinpointed to within 800–1800 metres.

3

Reception of alert signal by one of 14 worldwide stations

4 Rescue operation involving specialised units and often the military

P-3C Orion

The Lockheed P-3C Orion is an outstanding surveillance and anti-submarine aircraft and is equipped with a comprehensive range of sophisticated electronic sensors, including the Australian-designed Barra sonobuoy. It carries torpedoes for use against submarines and Harpoon missiles for ships. It is also able to lay mines at sea.

The Orions regularly patrol the coastline of Australia, looking for illegal activities in the Australian exclusive economic zone, as well as making long-range patrols into the Pacific, Indian and Southern oceans.

The aircraft is pressurised and air-conditioned for crew comfort on long missions. It can remain aloft for over 12 hours and sweep up to 250,000 square miles of ocean, sensing what is happening in the ocean, on the surface, and above it by day and night.

92 Wing, which operates the RAAF P-3C Orions, is based at RAAF Edinburgh in South Australia. Orion aircraft are continuously deployed on rotation at RMAF Butterworth in Malaysia.

P-3C Orion

Manufacturer	Lockheed Aircraft Corporation, USA
Engines	Four Allison T56 turboprop, each 4600 shaft horsepower
Airframe	Length 35.6 m; height 10.3 m
Wingspan	30.2 m
Weight	61 235 kg maximum
Speed	660 kmh
Range	Ferrying 7900 km
Ceiling	30 000 feet
Weapons	Harpoon missiles, torpedoes, mines
Avionics	Radar, acoustic processor, electronic support measures, infra-red detection system, central computer processing
Crew	Two pilots, two navigators, two flight engineers, five air electronics analysts

Air-Sea Rescue Kit contents

4	Marine solar stills
2	Torches
2	Pocket knives
1	Whistle
2	Signalling mirrors
10	Survival blankets
4	First-aid kits & manuals
	Insect repellent
	Sunscreen & anti-chap lipstick
8	Sets of sun goggles
3	Rolls of toilet paper
10	Litres of drinking water
4	Tubes of condensed milk
2	Packs of playing cards
24	Packs of survival rations
4	Air splints
4	Light luminescence
42	Drinking water bags
4	Emergency fishing kits
4	Packets of marine safety matches

Orion flight crew scan the water for signs of Thierry Dubois and Tony Bullimore. From left to right: Flight Engineer Peter Forrest, Flying Officer Paul Carpenter, Squadron Leader Alf Jonas (pilot) and Flight Engineer Tony McFadden.

One of five Orion crews involved in the search and rescue operation. Rear row, from left to right: WOff Tony Keogh, FlgOff Mick Durrant, FltLt Graham Nayler, Sgt Mark Kochenow, FltSgt Glen Richardson, Sgt Jamie Stirling. Front row: FltSgt Brett Morton, WOff Robert York, Capt Mike Houde, FltLt Ian Whyte. Absent from shot: FltLt Phil Buckley, LAC Matt Moore.

Orion crew, from left to right: FltLt Craig Simpson, WOff Robert York, FltLt Andrew Campbell, FlgOff Nicholas Platts, FltSgt Anthony McFadden, FltSgt Sean Judge, FltSgt Liam Craig, FltSgt Jason Powers, FltSgt Darren Sambell, FltSgt Trevor Grant, Sgt Jamie Stirling and at the front, FltLt Ian Whyte.

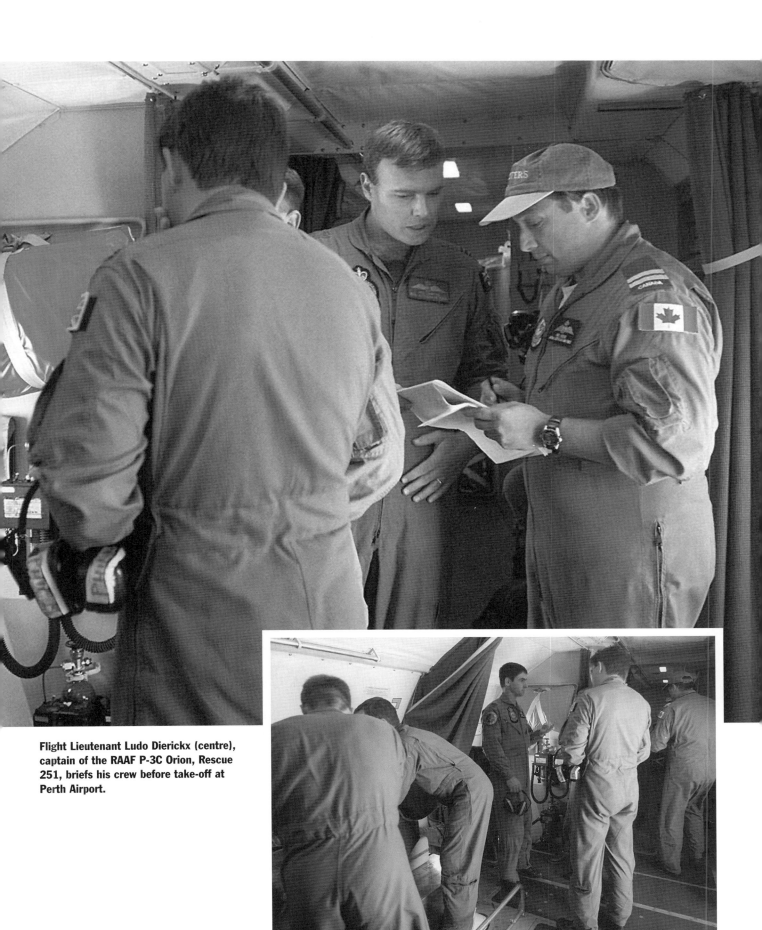

Flight Lieutenant Ludo Dierickx (centre), captain of the RAAF P-3C Orion, Rescue 251, briefs his crew before take-off at Perth Airport.

HMAS Adelaide

Captain Raydon Gates

Captain Raydon Gates joined the Royal Australian Naval College in 1972 and graduated in 1974. He undertook Operations and Warfare courses in the UK before returning to Australia to serve on HMAS *Stuart*, where in 1976 he gained his Bridge Watchdog qualifications. A posting as Executive Officer of HMAS *Swan* preceded his promotion to Commander and subsequent postings to the Joint Service Staff College and service in Australian Defence Force Headquarters, Canberra (HQADF). He served as Director of Surface and Air Warfare in Maritime Headquarters before his promotion to Captain on 1 January 1995. He assumed command of HMAS *Adelaide* in June 1995.

Guided Missile Frigates (FFGs)

The RAN operates six guided missile frigates of the Oliver Hazard Perry or FFG 7 class. This is the largest class of major surface combatant built in peacetime since the end of World War II. About 70 ships of this basic class have been built or are under construction around the world.

The first four ships, HMAS *Adelaide*, *Canberra*, *Sydney* and *Darwin* were built in the US, while the last two ships, *Melbourne* and *Newcastle*, were built at Williamstown in Victoria.

These ships introduced the minimum manning concept into the RAN and as such have a high degree of automation in their systems. Much of the maintenance of the ships' systems is done ashore rather than by the ship's company.

These ships are multi-role escorts with capabilities in air, surface and anti-submarine warfare (ASW). They were the first RAN escort ships to be equipped with a helicopter, as well as being the first RAN ships to be fitted with the Phalanx close-in air defence weapon system, the Harpoon anti-shipping missile and gas turbine propulsion.

The ship's principal weapon systems are the SM1 missile system, launching Standard and Harpoon missiles, 76 mm gun and two Mk 32 anti-submarine torpedo tubes for launching Mk 46 torpedoes. Each ship is also capable of embarking two Seahawk helicopters for ASW, surveillance and weapon-targeting tasks.

Seahawk

The Seahawk plays a crucial role in Australia's anti-submarine warfare programme. The Seahawk is an integrated part of defence strategies involving the Guided Missile Frigates. It carries a crew of three, and two torpedoes. It has a range of 525 nautical miles and can achieve a cruise speed of 140 knots.

The crew and support team from HS816 Squadron HMAS Adelaide Seahawk flight.

Lieutenant Commander Arthur Heather, officer in charge of the Seahawk helicopter flight involved in the rescue missions from HMAS Adelaide.

Rescued yachtsman
Thierry Dubois

AUSTRALIA

50°

Southern Ocean

ANTARCTICA

The rescue area, 1400 nautical miles
south-west of Perth.

Thierry Dubois
Clinging to Life

Rescuers guided by upturned yacht

French sailor Thierry Dubois on the stern of his capsized yacht, Pour Amnesty International, in heavy seas at 52 degrees latitude.

Flight Lieutenant Ludo Dierickx, captain of the Orion aircraft Rescue 251 on the search and rescue mission to find Dubois and Bullimore, said Dubois was found as soon as the plane arrived in the area. Flight Lieutenant Dierickx said Dubois was in high spirits when he saw the rescue plane.

'He was easy to spot and because the yacht was upturned and the keel was sticking right out of the water . . . to our joy we saw, on top of the upturned yacht, the survivor,' said Flight Lieutenant Dierickx.

The RAAF crew dropped a life raft to Dubois, however, Flight Lieutenant Dierickx said 12-metre seas and 60-knot winds made the task difficult. 'Visibility was only about one mile and the conditions were probably as bad as I've seen so far; they were quite rough and making our job taxing.'

Dubois was unable to get on a life raft dropped to him by the aircraft, and was still clinging to the upturned hull of his yacht.

Short on fuel, the first Orion craft was forced to head back to Perth. Dubois, meanwhile, waited anxiously for the second Orion aircraft, Rescue 252, to bring him aid.

Conditions in the area were worsening, with winds up to 60 knots, and the sailor was in 'a very serious situation.'

Dubois safe; hope for Bullimore

A stricken Thierry Dubois managed to get safely aboard a life raft after a second attempt to get survival gear to him succeeded. Dubois got on board the raft just before 7.44 p.m. (EST) after it was dropped by the second of two RAAF Orion aircraft that flew to the scene from Perth on 6 January. The first raft dropped by Rescue 251 four hours earlier was swamped by high seas. The Frenchman had been clinging to the hull of his upturned yacht for about 24 hours before finally securing the raft.

Dubois faces a wait of nearly three days on board the life raft until the RAN frigate HMAS *Adelaide*, which left Perth last night, reaches him.

The life raft carries with it enough life-preserving equipment and food to last for almost a week.

An RAAF spokesman said the crew of RAAF P-3C Orion, Rescue 252, also spotted the second yacht, Englishman Tony Bullimore's *Global Exide Challenger*, about 60 kilometres away from the Frenchman. The *Global Exide Challenger* was upright but listing. There was no sign of Bullimore.

Meanwhile, HMAS *Adelaide* has been steaming to the area at 26 knots, faster than expected. This is using fuel at a very high rate. The tanker HMAS *Westralia* is under direction to meet the frigate to enable it to refuel.

Unable to secure the first life raft, Dubois waits on the hull of his overturned yacht Pour Amnesty International.

Dubois had been clinging to the hull of his upturned yacht for about 24 hours before finally securing a life raft dropped by the RAAF.

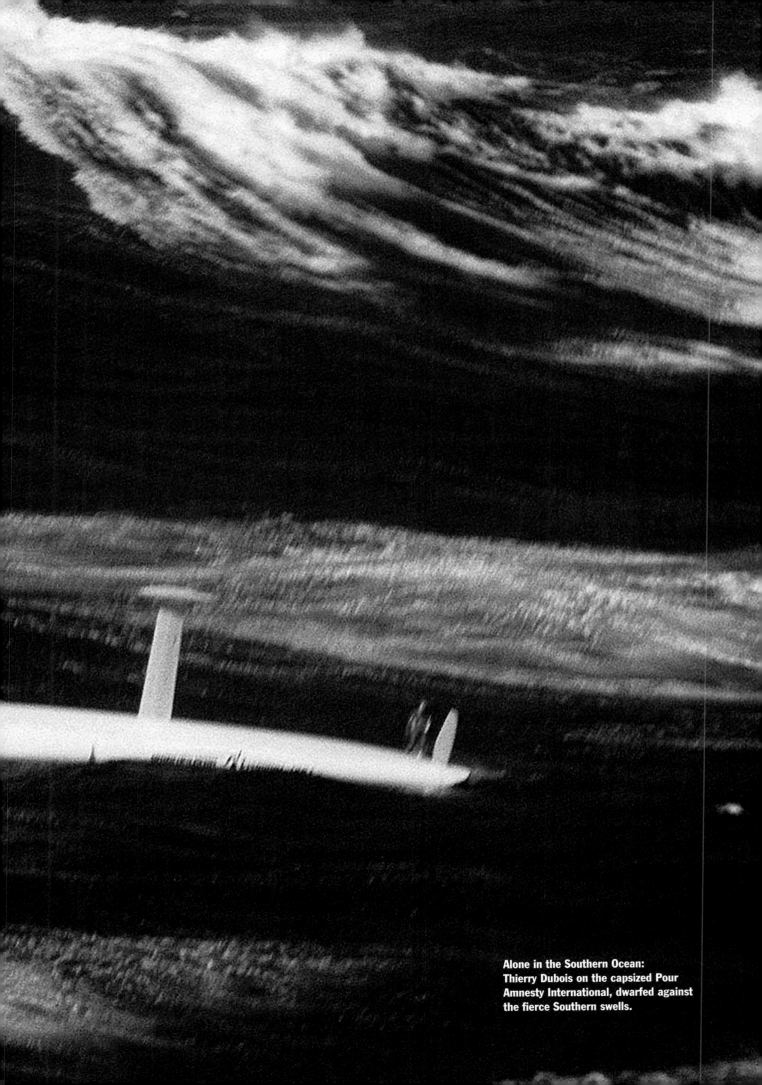

Alone in the Southern Ocean:
Thierry Dubois on the capsized Pour
Amnesty International, dwarfed against
the fierce Southern swells.

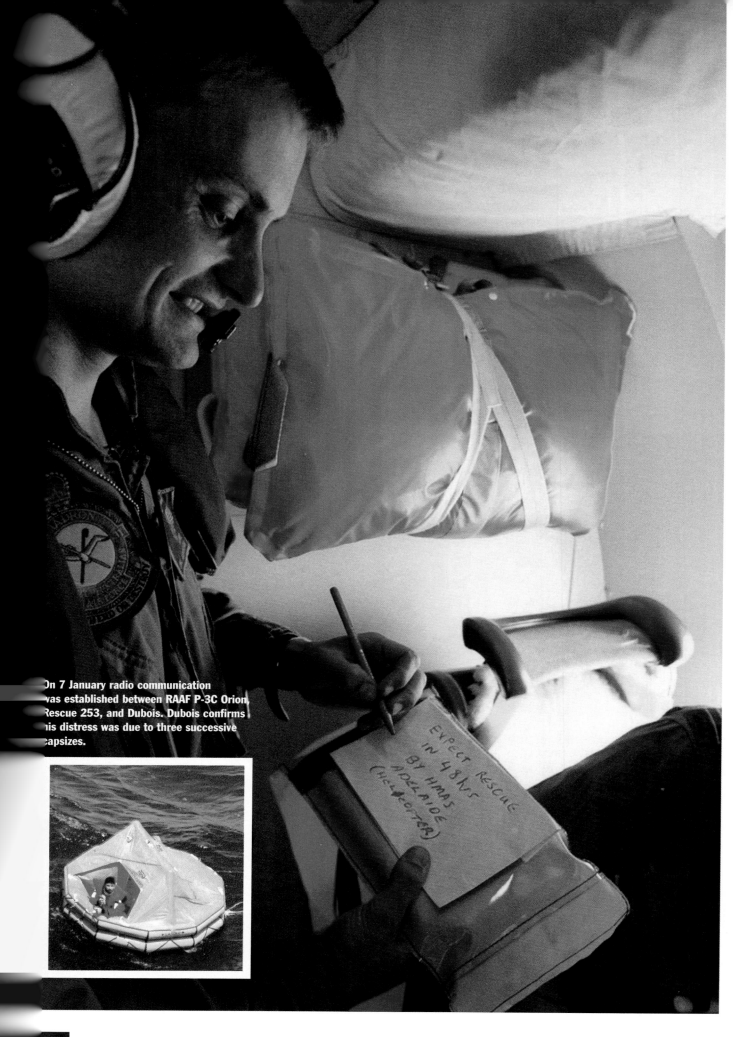

On 7 January radio communication was established between RAAF P-3C Orion, Rescue 253, and Dubois. Dubois confirms his distress was due to three successive capsizes.

EXPECT RESCUE IN 48 HRS BY HMAS ADELAIDE (HELICOPTER)

Plucked from Southern waters

Dubois was rescued and evacuated from his life raft by a RAN Seahawk helicopter and taken to HMAS *Adelaide*. He seemed to be in good condition, suffering just mild hypothermia.

Dubois had only praise for those who saved him. 'They want to congratulate me, but I want to congratulate them. This is really a problem. I don't need congratulations. This (ceremony) is for them. This search was so fantastic.'

Why Dubois's yacht rolled over

Rogue wave

• Rogue wave approaches from a 90° angle from the rest of the waves, knocking the boat on its side.
• Boats entered in the race are required to be self-righting and so it should have righted itself. It is possible that modifications to the boat could have been made, reducing this ability.

Self-righting

• When a racing boat is sailing down wind (running) the water ballast tanks would be empty to make the boat lighter. The only way to activate the tanks is from inside the hull of the boat.
• The wide beam of the boat makes it harder to self-right.
• The small cabin means there is less air trapped that could assist in righting.
• After a boat has been upside down for some time the mast will fill with water making it heavy.

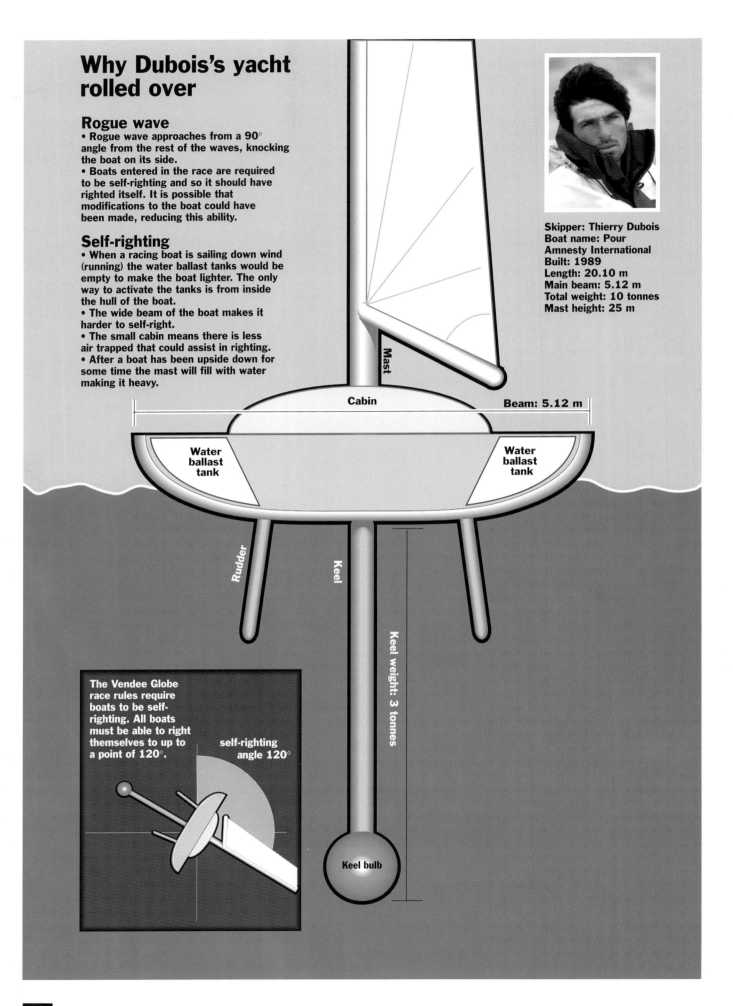

Skipper: Thierry Dubois
Boat name: Pour Amnesty International
Built: 1989
Length: 20.10 m
Main beam: 5.12 m
Total weight: 10 tonnes
Mast height: 25 m

Mast

Cabin

Beam: 5.12 m

Water ballast tank

Water ballast tank

Rudder

Keel

Keel weight: 3 tonnes

Keel bulb

The Vendee Globe race rules require boats to be self-righting. All boats must be able to right themselves to up to a point of 120°.

self-righting angle 120°

'We would do It again'

The Minister for Defence, Mr Ian McLachlan, today acknowledged the efforts of the Australian Defence Force personnel in mounting the successful rescue of French yachtsman Thierry Dubois and the search for the missing British yachtsman Tony Bullimore in the Southern Ocean.

'All of Australia is aware of the efforts of the Royal Australian Air Force, the Royal Australian Navy and the Australian Maritime Safety Authority to rescue the yachtsmen from their capsized yachts, *Pour Amnesty International* and *Global Exide Challenger*,' McLachlan said.

'Mr Dubois is very fortunate to have survived such a mishap so far from land and in such adverse conditions. He was rescued from a life raft at approximately 7.15 a.m. EST by a RAN Seahawk helicopter and flown to HMAS *Adelaide*. The search is now concentrating on locating Mr Bullimore.

'We commend the crews of the P-3C Orion aircraft which flew the missions from RAAF base Edinburgh in South Australia, plus the sailors, under Captain Raydon Gates on board HMAS *Adelaide*, which sailed from Perth on this mission.

'Many of those involved in the rescue were recalled from leave to take part in this operation. We acknowledge their dedication and thank their families and loved ones for their understanding and support.

'The role of those more indirectly involved in mounting the search missions must also be acknowledged – the ADF and civilian personnel who provided the 24-hour control, command and support arrangements.

'They are to be congratulated for their contributions to this long-range rescue effort, and for the earlier successful rescue of another French yachtsman, Raphael Dinelli.'

The Defence Minister said that the principal focus of such operations was the saving of life, but there were benefits also from the lessons learnt from the operation and review of rescue procedures. These required examination for the most practical way of improving our response time for future eventualities. Debriefings would identify possible improvements in techniques.

'We have done what is required, and we would do it again, whenever necessary,' McLachlan said.

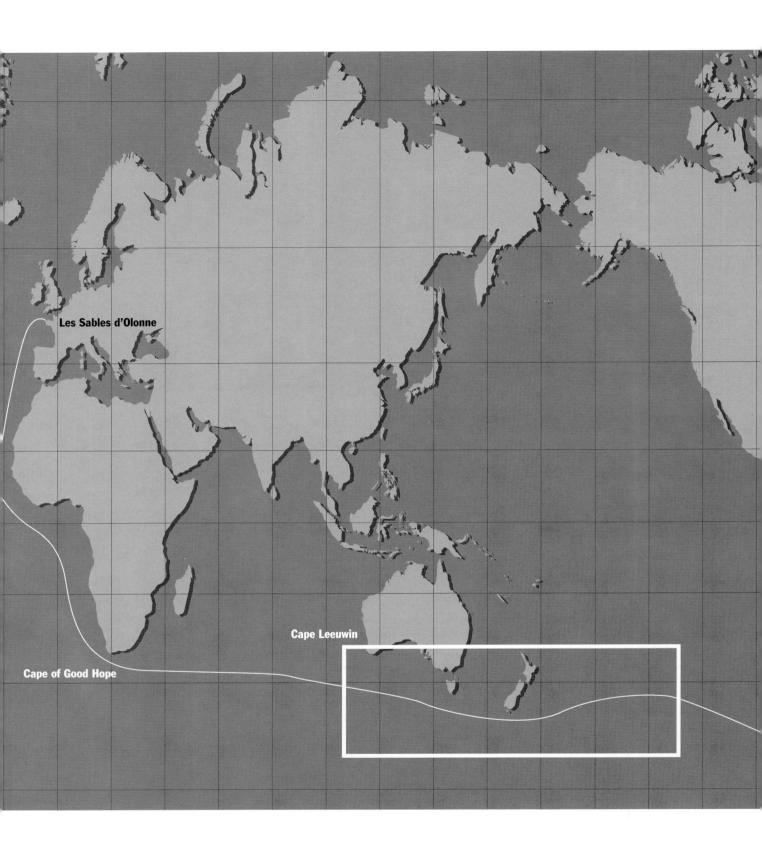

Les Sables d'Olonne

Cape Leeuwin

Cape of Good Hope

The race in progress

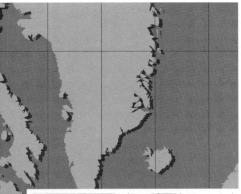

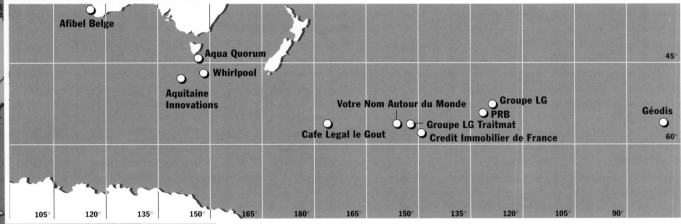

Afibel Belge

Aqua Quorum

Whirlpool

Aquitaine
Innovations

Votre Nom Autour du Monde

Groupe LG

PRB

Groupe LG Traitmat

Cafe Legal le Gout

Credit Immobilier de France

Géodis

45°

60°

105°   120°   135°   150°   165°   180°   165°   150°   135°   120°   105°   90°

Growing concern for fourth yachtsman

Leader of the Vendee Globe race, Frenchman Christophe Augin, passed through Drake Passage, between South America and Antarctica, today. As Augin heads north on the homeward stretch, the other competitors are scattered between Australia and Chile.

A fourth competitor, Canadian Gerry Roufs, is missing south-west of Cape Horn. Roufs was Augin's nearest competitor, however, race organisers have lost track of the satellite beacon on board his yacht *Groupe LG*, and he is not responding to radio calls. Race organisers have requested Isabelle Autissier to turn back to help search for Roufs. Autissier herself was rescued by the RAN and RAAF two years ago. Because she was forced to seek help earlier in this race, she is not officially a competitor in the 1996–97 challenge.

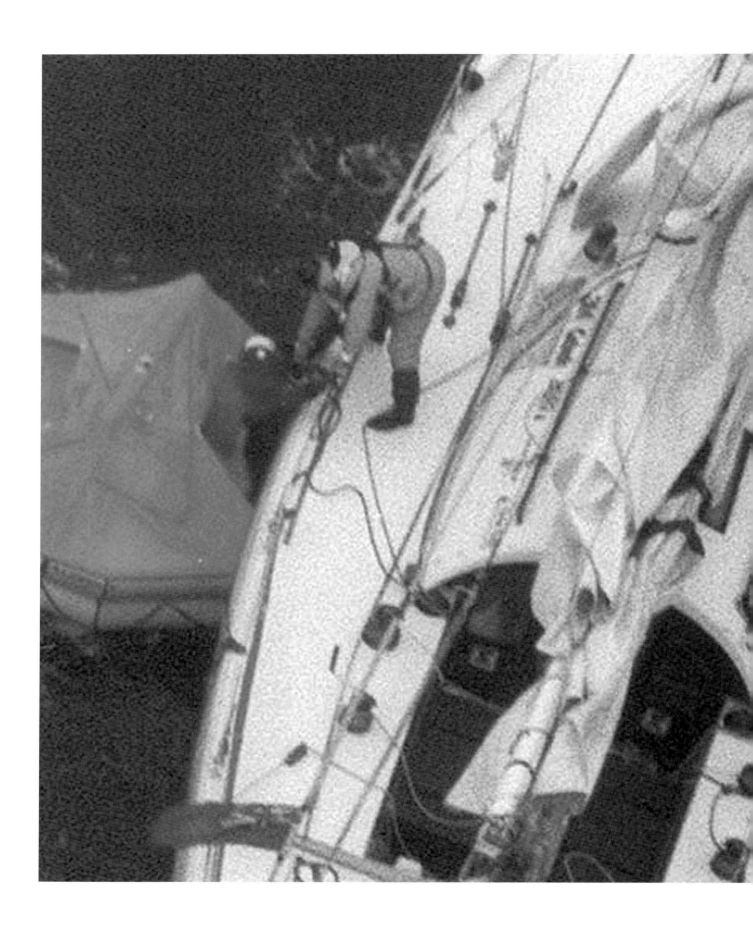

The latitude debate

The Roaring Forties and Furious Fifties of the Southern Hemisphere are the areas between the latitudes of 40 and 60 degrees south, where the prevailing winds blow from the west. These waters are well known by sailors for their strong, often gale-force winds throughout the year, which are relatively unrestricted by land mass. In light of the recent rescues of yachtsmen in difficulty from the Southern Ocean, organisers of events such as the Vendee Globe round-the-world yacht race have been called upon to rethink their routes to improve the safety of competitors.

While sailors used materials such as carbon fibre to build lighter and faster yachts, these might not be as safe for conditions encountered in such southern latitudes. The rescued yachtsmen are discussing the engineering of stronger, safer yachts that can right themselves in the event of bad weather.

Race enthusiasts, however are quick to point out that many of the early explorers sailed latitudes of 50 to 55 degrees south, and early shipping companies also undertook such routes for fast passages because they were usually the shortest way to go and provided the strongest, most consistent winds.

Explorers of the sixteenth to nineteenth centuries achieved their journeys with the barest navigational aids and no communication equipment. In comparison, today's sailors have greatly reduced risks.

It is interesting, too, to remember that European settlement of the 'Great Southern Land' is due to the courageous efforts of early explorers sailing uncharted areas.

Your money or your life?

What price a human life? In a week that saw three veteran yachtsmen lose their crafts and run up a substantial rescue bill, some people are questioning the costs involved.

The rescue operations in the Southern Ocean in January 1997 included members of the RAN, the RAAF and about a hundred ground staff. They coordinated a series of searches and supply drops, rescue missions that involved a navy frigate and a diverted merchant vessel, and helicopter rescue bids. All in all, an estimated bill that runs into the millions.

There is general admiration for the skills and professionalism of the Defence Force, which can justify such rescue missions as training exercises. There is compassion for those in danger. Most people recognise that the value of a human life is not measured in dollars, and that Australia's responsibilities in this matter are not only to its own citizens. However, the Australian government is appealing to race organisers to pay more attention to safety, and to consider safer routes.

Tony Bullimore
Miracle Survivor

Hopes of finding 58-year-old race competitor Tony Bullimore are considered high. Bullimore's capsized yacht, *Global Exide Challenger*, was spotted yesterday by search aircraft. Rescuers suspect the Englishman may be imprisoned in the upturned hull of his yacht about 55 nautical miles south of Dubois's life raft. Reports from the yacht's British designer indicate that if Bullimore is in the hull, and it has been made sea-proof, he should have up to six days of air.

Meanwhile, workers in a Sydney shipyard are trying to cut through a hull similar to the *Global Exide Challenger's* to see how best to open it. The results will be radioed to HMAS *Adelaide*.

'I knew conditions were rough, but he is very experienced and a very tough guy. If anyone can get through this, I know he will,' said his wife, Lalel Bullimore.

All attempts to locate Bullimore either on or near the *Global Exide Challenger* by the RAAF crews were unsuccessful. However at 11.30 p.m. on 8 January, RAAF P-3C Orion, Rescue 259, depicted regular tapping sounds coming from beneath the hull.

'I knew conditions were rough, but he is very experienced and a very tough guy. If anyone can get through this, I know he will.'

'I may never, in the time I have got left, ever have the chance to do it again.'

An old-style adventurer

Tony Bullimore may well have come from an ordinary family in the English seaside town of Southend-on-Sea, but he is an old-style adventurer who has led an extraordinary life.

Bullimore has been a fortune hunter in Africa and once dreamed of driving through the Sahara. He then decided that oceans were a bigger challenge than deserts, and turned his dreams to single-handed yachting.

After 27 Atlantic crossings Bullimore is regarded as one of Britain's most experienced sailors. The Vendee Globe is Bullimore's first attempt at non-stop circumnavigation, but he brings to the race a wealth of experience. He has sailed more than 400,000 kilometres and was named joint yachtsman of the year with his boat designer after winning the 1985 Round Britain and Round Europe races in an 18-metre trimaran, *Toria*.

He had also experienced danger first-hand. During a 1976 trans-Atlantic race he was rescued from his life raft by an oil tanker after *Toria* burst into flames. In 1989 he was skippering a yacht that flipped over during trials, killing one of the crew.

He saw the Vendee Globe solo yacht race as the major challenge of his life, and said in a pre-race interview: 'I may never, in the time I have got left, ever have the chance to do it again. Of the few things left on this Earth that I want to do, the Vendee Globe represents the major race, the major challenge. So I will do it.'

The rescue area,
3300 km off the coast of Australia.

Bullimore built the *Global Exide Challenger* knowing that he would have to depend on it to get him through the Vendee Globe challenge. The race specifications required that the yacht be self-righting and unsinkable, but not for one moment did he think that his survival would go so far down to the wire. Nor did he expect the keel, a replacement part that he did not make, to snap off as it did and cause the craft to overturn.

Photographic evidence suggests that the Global Exide Challenger hit a submerged object as the yacht flew down the face of a cresting swell. Bullimore was below deck in the galley at the moment of impact.

The Modern Sailor's Technology

Tony Bullimore's yacht had the latest technology that could plot his position to within 100 metres anywhere in the world, 24 hours a day.

HF (High Frequency) Radio
For long-range voice communications; $5000.

Weather Fax
Receives copies of daily weather maps for the area the yacht is sailing in; $3000.

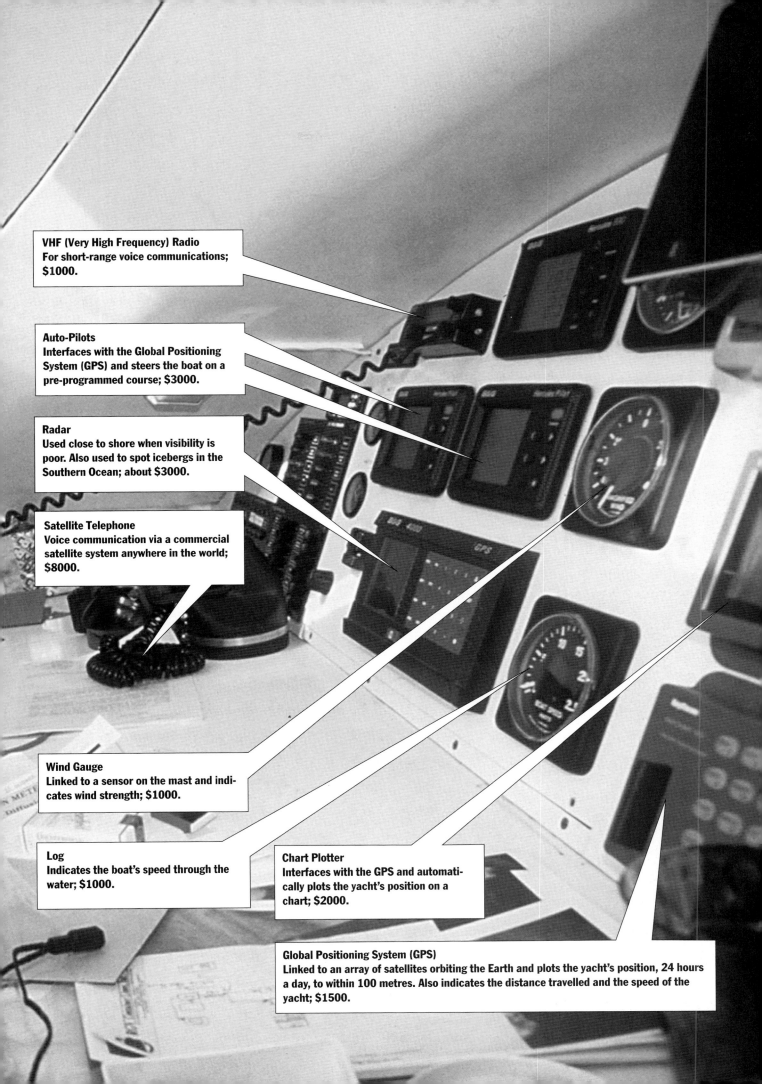

VHF (Very High Frequency) Radio
For short-range voice communications;
$1000.

Auto-Pilots
Interfaces with the Global Positioning
System (GPS) and steers the boat on a
pre-programmed course; $3000.

Radar
Used close to shore when visibility is
poor. Also used to spot icebergs in the
Southern Ocean; about $3000.

Satellite Telephone
Voice communication via a commercial
satellite system anywhere in the world;
$8000.

Wind Gauge
Linked to a sensor on the mast and indicates wind strength; $1000.

Log
Indicates the boat's speed through the
water; $1000.

Chart Plotter
Interfaces with the GPS and automati-
cally plots the yacht's position on a
chart; $2000.

Global Positioning System (GPS)
Linked to an array of satellites orbiting the Earth and plots the yacht's position, 24 hours
a day, to within 100 metres. Also indicates the distance travelled and the speed of the
yacht; $1500.

A sign of life

The rhythm of the tapping indicated the beat was human and not mechanical.

EXIDE CHALLENGER

33

Flight Lieutenant Ludo Dierickx (left) and
sonar operator Flight Sergeant Liam Craig
used sophisticated equipment to detect
tapping sounds from the capsized yacht

9 January 1997

In those seconds after he heard
the collision, Bullimore would
have felt the yacht begin to roll.
As it did, he would have tried to
struggle to his feet from his sitting position at the chart table.
As the yacht continued down, its
mast and rigging would have hit
the water. According to yachting
author Jim Murrant the elapsed
time between impact and capsize

four seconds.

Tapping sounds that lasted
for 90 seconds were picked
up from the hull of the *Global
Exide Challenger* by sonobuoy
after electronic underwater noise
makers were dropped into the
surrounding waters. The rhythm
of the tapping indicated to ana-
lysts the beat was man-made,
and not a natural sound.

Precious life beneath the hull

His greatest enemies were cold, hunger and dehydration. Sustaining his mental and physical health was critical to Bullimore's survival.

Bullimore said he had heard the searching RAAF Orions but was unsure if the noise was caused by the sea. He feared that if he dived out of his cabin to a false alarm he might be further endangered.

He had planned to make a hole in the hull and fire rockets if he heard any more machine noise. After so many hours under the hull his spirits were flagging. Papers and equipment were being sucked out of the cabin.

Outside this cocoon, the storm that caused the *Global Exide Challenger* to founder still raged. With winds of 60 knots and swells approaching the height of a five-storey building, the noise battering Bullimore would have been intense. A wave of 12 metres will have three or more metres of broken water at its peak.

This natural cacophony would have continued, unabated, for as long as the slate-grey skies of the Antarctic unleashed winds of Force 8 strength and beyond.

Inside the main cabin, three metres long and two metres wide, it was pitch dark. The water had reached knee level at one end and was waist deep at the other.

Bullimore could just stand on what was formerly the roof and, with effort, reach from one side of the yacht to the other. He had no torch, a limited supply of water and some chocolate as he sheltered in the hammock suspended from what had been the cabin floor. Water poured in and out in what he described as 'a Niagara Falls effect' through a window ripped out by the force of the storm.

His greatest enemies were cold, hunger and dehydration. Sustaining his mental and pysical health was critical to Bullimore's survival.

Safe at last

The chances of staying alive in the waters of the Southern Ocean could be measured in minutes.

The upturned hull of Global Exide Challenger, lying half-immersed in the water.

A crew of rescuers from HMAS *Adelaide*, including divers and engineers, hammered on the upturned hull, hoping to drill and cut their way through it. But this proved unnecessary when Bullimore bobbed up alongside the hull in his orange immersion suit, to the surprise and joy of all hands on the frigate.

At first the six-man rescue crew in the seven-metre Rigid Inflatable Boat (RIB) could not see Bullimore, who was on the far side of his grey-and-white hull. The temperature of the water was –2°C and the danger of dying from exposure in the sub-Antarctic waters was considerable. Medical information that was circulated earlier had shown that the chances of anyone staying alive in the waters of the Southern Ocean, even with full immersion suit, could be measured in minutes.

'I'm coming out . . .

‘When I saw this ship standing there and this plane going over the top and these couple of guys peering over an upturned hull, it was heaven, absolute heaven.’

It was the 'illogical knocking' that convinced Bullimore to risk swimming for safety after spending four days entombed in his upturned yacht.

‘Bang, bang-be bang bang, funny old bangs. I thought, "Well, that's a bloody human being." What I heard was like heaven.’

‘I dived to the other end of the boat. I'm screaming, "I'm coming out, I'm coming out",’ Bullimore recounted.

‘When I saw this ship standing there and this plane going over the top and these couple of guys peering over an upturned hull, it was heaven, absolute heaven.’

I'm coming out!'

Tony Bullimore swims towards the
RAN RIB in the sub-Antarctic waters
of the Southern Ocean.

Born all over again

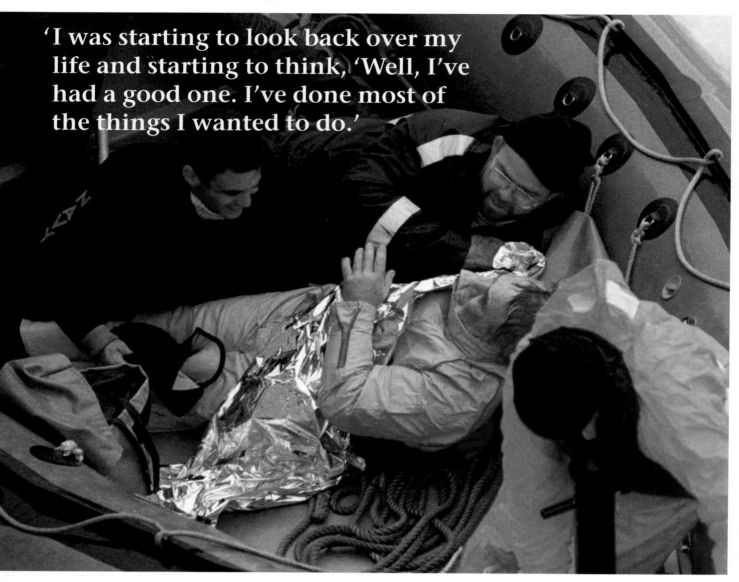

'I was starting to look back over my life and starting to think, 'Well, I've had a good one. I've done most of the things I wanted to do.'

Leading Seaman Clearance Diver Alan Rub (left) and Chief Petty Officer Peter Wicker comfort Tony Bullimore after they plucked him from the freezing waters of the Southern Ocean.

Bullimore was pulled onto the RIB, covered in a silver foil blanket, his head cradled in a sailor's arms. As the runabout was winched onto HMAS *Adelaide*, he called out: 'Are we on board? Did you get a picture of my boat?'

Bullimore was not wearing gloves and was holding his damaged hands. He also had a black eye. Sailors struggled to calm him as he tried to see what was happening. He was suffering from hypothermia, frostbite, cuts and bruising, and had lost the tip of one finger in a hatch.

Dr David Wright, who attended to Dubois and Bullimore, said their survival was due to their tenacity and the protection rendered by

their immersion suits.

Bullimore was swathed in blankets and taken to the sick bay. An hour later he was keen to tell of his experiences.

'I never really thought I'd come this far,' he said, recalling the time he spent alone in the hull.

'I was starting to look back over my life and starting to think, "Well, I've had a good one. I've done most of the things I wanted to do. I've had a good life."

'I've become more human in these past six days. I won't be so rude to people . . . I'll be much more of a gentleman. And I'll listen to people a lot more. I feel it's like being born all over again.'

Rigid Inflatable Boat (RIB)

The dramatic rescue in raging seas and high winds was made by Australian navy sailors and divers who sped to Bullimore's upturned yacht in a Rigid Inflatable Boat (RIB). The RAN selected this craft for use at sea because of its versatility and relative light weight (1958 kg) compared with wooden or steel boats of a similar size. It is easily manoeuvred and withstands weathering. Once crews are properly trained in its use, the RIB is considered a better option in many circumstances faced by the navy at sea than conventional boats. The 7.2-metre RIB is used mainly to transport personnel, light stores and as a fast-response vessel. It can carry up to 25 people at speeds in excess of 31 knots.

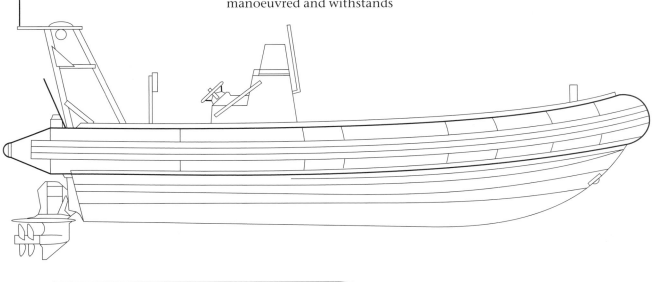

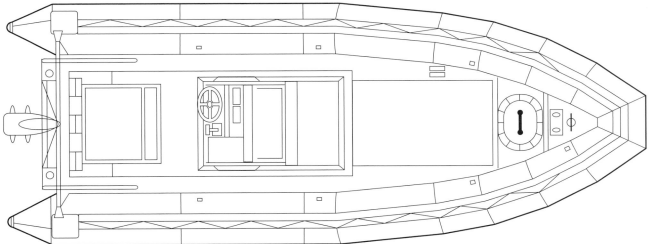

Purpose	To transport personnel, light stores and act as a fast-response vessel or as a seaboat
Construction	GRP hull, Hypalon tubes
Length	7.2 m
Beam	2.74 m
Draught	0.53 m
Weight (less fuel and crew)	1958 kg
Fuel capacity	200 litres
Machinery	Volvo Penta AQAD41/DP sterndrive
Speed	31+ knots
Endurance	5 hours at 15 knots
Capacity	18 persons (max); 25 persons (emergency)
Manufacturer	Zodiac (Australia) Pty Ltd

Looking at life

'When I looked over at the *Adelaide*,
I could only get the tremendous
ecstasy that I was looking at life . . .
It was heaven, absolute heaven.'

The RIB carrying Tony Bullimore
pulls alongside the frigate HMAS Adelaide.

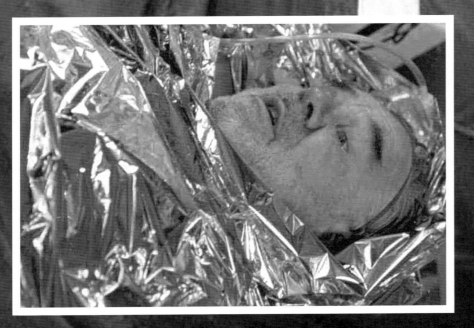

Suffering from hypothermia, frostbite, cuts and bruising – but alive.

The rescue crew aboard the RIB comfort Bullimore, and wrap him in an insulating silver foil blanket.

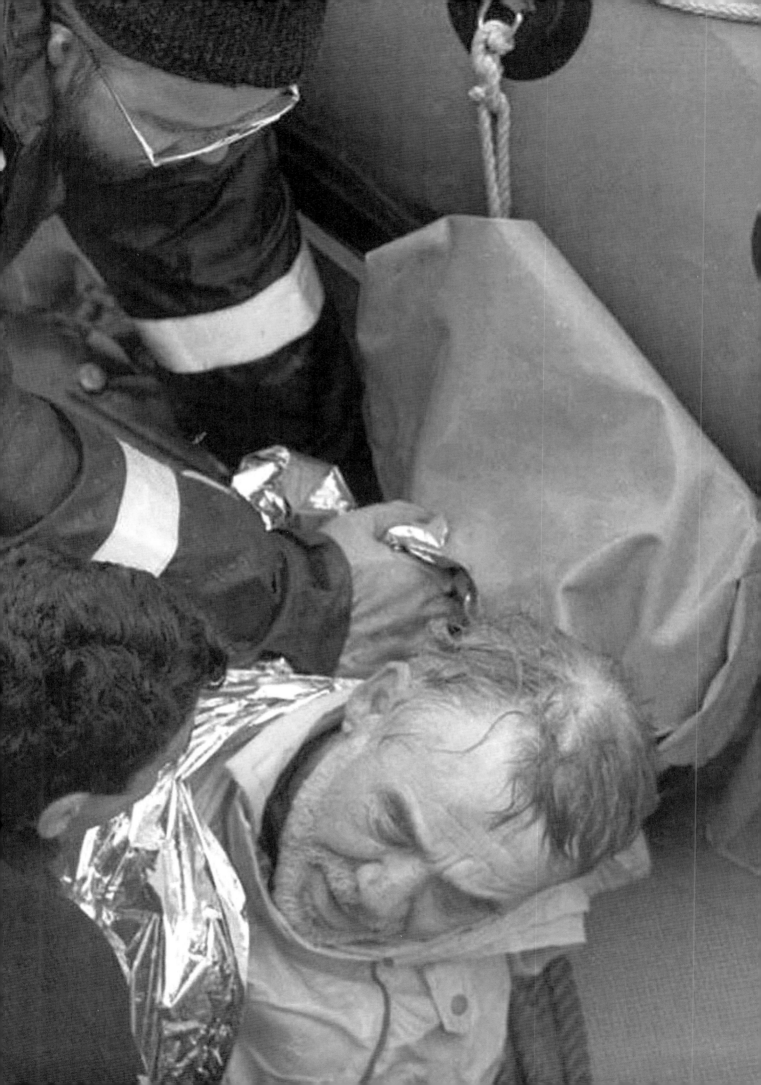

A race against time and ocean

The rescue of Tony Bullimore and Thierry Dubois is one of the most complex rescue operations ever carried out by Australia's Defence Force.

Maritime commander Rear Admiral Christopher Oxenbould assembled a team of RAN strategists to observe the navy's role. Two RAN ships, four RAAF P-3C Orions, a helicopter and hundreds of defence and civilian personnel were pressed into service for an operation that had one imperative: to get down south fast, almost as far as Antarctica, before the seas and the sub-zero temperatures claimed the lives of the two sailors.

The RAN's role was part of a huge operation coordinated by the Australian Maritime Safety Authority and Airservices Australia. Seeking advice from civilian boat designers and yachting experts, the RAN assembled both civilian and military expertise, gathering crucial information that would help the sailors combat the extreme conditions. The rescues were therefore conducted by fax and telephone, and with on-the-spot instruction. Details were sent to the *Adelaide* to be studied by those who would actually be put to sea and perform the rescue.

HMAS *Adelaide* and the supply vessel, HMAS *Westralia*, were already at sea and would have to make do with whatever equipment they had on board. The RAAF was already flying sorties over the rescue area.

The RAN knew that speed was crucial once Bullimore was found. They tracked down the *Challenger's* designers in London who faxed

them a hand-drawn plan of the hull, indicating where Bullimore was most likely to be, and how long he could survive. RAN personnel practised on the substance and faxed to HMAS *Adelaide*.

'It felt like a scene from "Apollo 13",' says Captain Moffitt. 'It was too late to get equipment to HMAS *Adelaide* and the crew had to make do with what they had on board. We spent a lot of brain power trialling the material we got and sending the latest information to the captain of the *Adelaide*.'

The race against time and the elements began at 51 minutes past midnight on 6 January, when emergency services picked up four beacons from two yachts off the coast of Australia. At 1.20 a.m., the RAAF base at Edinburgh near Adelaide was told P-3C Orion aircraft from 92 Wing would be required for the search.

Within minutes Squadron Leader Vic Lewkowski was told to assemble a crew for Orion craft to fly to Western Australia. By the end of the week, six air crews, totalling more than 70 personnel and a 17-member maintenance squadron from 92 Wing, were running and supporting sorties into the Southern Ocean from a base at Perth Airport.

Flight Lieutenant Ludo Dierickx was called at home at 3 a.m. Three hours later, he was captain on the first Orion to leave on the four-hour trip to Perth, where they quickly refuelled, and headed for the search area. Wind speed was over 100 kilometres an hour; the seas were throwing up ten-metre swells; the air temperature was 1°C and the water was about

Reaching Dubois

7.30 a.m. yesterday: Seahawk takes off from HMAS Adelaide to pick up Dubois about 50 nautical miles away.

8.20 a.m.: Helicopter reaches Dubois and lowers crewman. The two are then winched back to the helicopter.

5°C. They were flying so low at times that the salt spray became encrusted on the windows.

At 12.51 a.m. on 6 January discussions were held about involving the RAN. Less than two hours later, the RAN's Captain Moffitt was telephoned at home and told the Vendee Globe rescue mission was on, and that the *Adelaide* had a suitable helicopter for the task.

Aboard the *Adelaide*, Executive Officer Jim Manson briefed boat crews as they were about to leave: 'None of us are trained salvage experts,' he said. 'I don't want

Drama below the 50th parallel

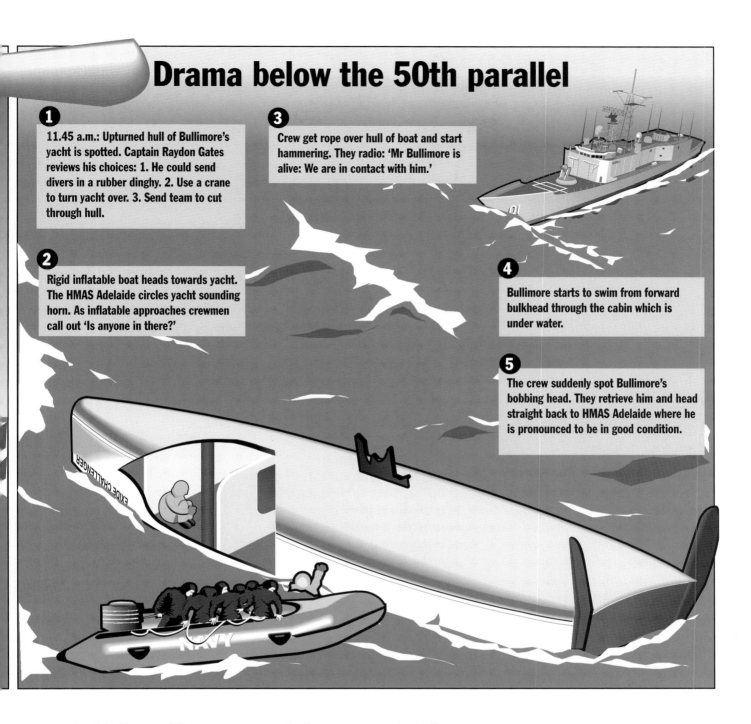

1
11.45 a.m.: Upturned hull of Bullimore's yacht is spotted. Captain Raydon Gates reviews his choices: 1. He could send divers in a rubber dinghy. 2. Use a crane to turn yacht over. 3. Send team to cut through hull.

2
Rigid inflatable boat heads towards yacht. The HMAS Adelaide circles yacht sounding horn. As inflatable approaches crewmen call out 'Is anyone in there?'

3
Crew get rope over hull of boat and start hammering. They radio: 'Mr Bullimore is alive: We are in contact with him.'

4
Bullimore starts to swim from forward bulkhead through the cabin which is under water.

5
The crew suddenly spot Bullimore's bobbing head. They retrieve him and head straight back to HMAS Adelaide where he is pronounced to be in good condition.

any misguided heroes. We are going there to save lives but in doing so not endanger ourselves.'

The Orion crew, Rescue 251, found Thierry Dubois within 15 minutes of arriving in the search area. They had to drop two sets of life rafts after the first one failed to reach him, and then went in search of Bullimore. They scanned two-thirds of the search area before reaching their minimum reserve of fuel, which forced them to return to Perth. The second Orion on the scene found the *Global Exide Challenger*.

As the rescue crew, including divers and engineers, prepared to cut their way into the *Global Exide Challenger's* hull at 11.45 a.m. on 9 January, Bullimore swam out from beneath the boat and was brought to safety.

Elation spread through the entire defence force. 'We're all over the moon,' said Colonel Andrew Reynolds. 'Our mission was to go out and rescue two yachtsmen and that's precisely what we've done and we are so pleased about that.'

No ordinary person
Sea Lion

'The kind of person who takes part in a solo yacht race like this is going to be someone very sure of their own skills and experience and who lives a bit on the edge.'

Tony Bullimore insists that he is just an ordinary man, but his survival has been anything but ordinary. The story he told journalists aboard the guided-missile frigate HMAS *Adelaide* within hours of the rescue spoke volumes about his dogged determination and resourcefulness.

He had dived at least a dozen times into the pitch-black icy water that filled his boat in a vain bid to untether the life raft that was tangled in its stowage on the deck.

Between each dive he returned, his lungs almost bursting, to a tiny air pocket in the sleeping cabin. There he would dry and warm himself as best as he could, and curl up in a makeshift hammock that he had knocked up out of cargo netting. Then he would try again.

He calculated his odds of survival as not very good, but worked out when to switch a beacon from emergency to distress, and when to make regular noises in response to electronic noise makers in the ocean, to give rescuers vital signs that he was still alive.

When he heard a rescue plane, presence of mind told him that it would be better to stay put and trust that his boat had been spotted rather than show himself and risk not being seen. He realised that once he had dived out of the craft he would never again be able to return to his dark, eerie shelter and the relative comfort of his cradle.

British survival experts claim Bullimore survived his four-day ordeal as much through mental determination and the ability to keep a clear head as through physical stamina. A clinical psychologist, Eileen Kennedy, said he must be a special individual: 'This chap is no ordinary person like you or me . . . He's an experienced solo sailor, used to relying on himself in stressful, dangerous situations.'

'The kind of person who takes part in a solo yacht race like this is going to be someone very sure of their own skills and experience and who lives a bit on the edge.'

Inside Tony Bullimore's 'Tomb'

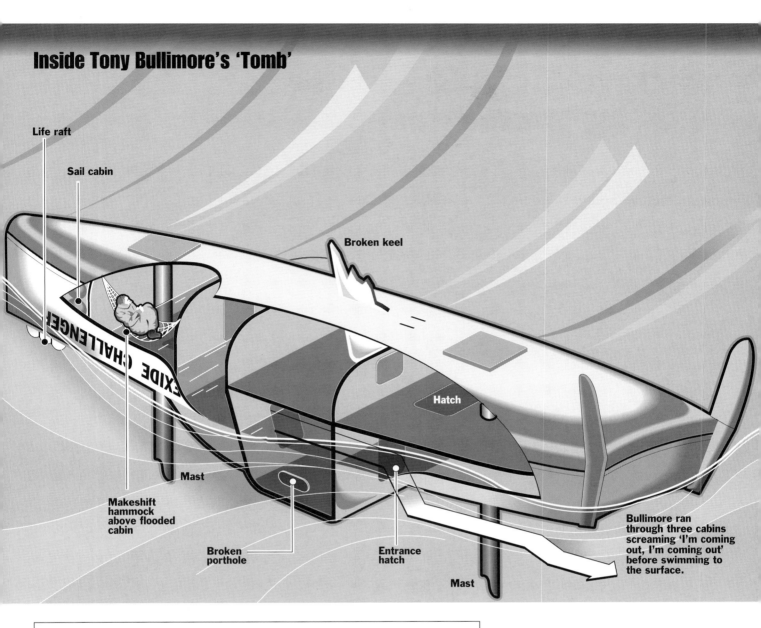

Life raft

Sail cabin

Broken keel

EXIDE CHALLENGER

Hatch

Mast

Makeshift
hammock
above flooded
cabin

Broken
porthole

Entrance
hatch

Mast

Bullimore ran
through three cabins
screaming 'I'm coming
out, I'm coming out'
before swimming to
the surface.

How Bullimore Survived

1 Stayed calm and activated distress signals, which set off a four-day
rescue operation.

2 Wore an anti-freeze immersion suit to minimise heat loss.

3 Changed the distress signal manually to alert rescuers to his presence.

4 Made himself secure in the sealed sleeping compartment where air supply
would hold for about 145 hours.

5 Built a makeshift hammock from cargo netting and strapped himself into it to
keep dry above a flooded cabin.

6 Removed instruments on surfaces of the boat to get access to outside air.

7 Rapped on the inside of the hull for 90 seconds after noise-making devices
and sonobuoys were dropped next to the submerged yacht.

8 Tapped in response to electronic noise makers dropped from an Orion.

9 Let off a small personal beacon, which rescuers described as another piece
to the 'jigsaw puzzle'.

10 Waited until the Zodiac crew was alongside before risking exposure in
near-freezing waters.

'Fantastic': new rescues bring joy to a race hero

The surge of elation from the recovery of their fellow Vendee Globe competitors reached the group at the heart of the earlier rescue effort as they left Hobart.

'Fantastic,' a smiling Peter Goss said as he prepared, with some apprehension, to resume the race. He was well out of touch with the rest of the fleet should he need help himself.

'Really? The Englishman too?' said Raphael Dinelli's partner, Virginie Glory at Hobart airport.

Two weeks after Goss rescued Dinelli in the Southern Ocean, the two parted at lunchtime on the Hobart waterfront. Goss was preparing his yacht to resume racing. Dinelli took a launch out with a parting gift of pizza for Goss, who has not been able to leave his yacht *Aqua Quorum*. Dinelli had said earlier he would say to Goss: 'Good luck, and my heart is with your heart.'

Goss had remained optimistic that the fighting spirit of the race would mean survival for Thierry Dubois and Tony Bullimore.

He welcomed the news of the rescue as a wonderful parting gift. 'It was a very good find,' he said.

Now with most of the race fleet more than 3000 nautical miles ahead of him, Goss admitted 'I'm a bit more vulnerable now. I'll have to approach it accordingly. But I'll be all right.'

Goss had remained optimistic that the fighting spirit of the race would mean survival for Thierry Dubois and Tony Bullimore.

A survivor's tale

'I started asking myself, "Am I really preparing my grave?" I really believe I was just on the brink. I got to the point where I was thinking in hours.'

'One minute I'm sitting there with me old cup of tea and the next thing is bang — and the keel pops off. The boat went over so quick . . . I was frightened because it was taking a terrible battering. I thought: "This is it, I'm really in the s... now".

'I wanted to get to the life raft because I was frightened that anybody who would come might just look and say, "Ah, it's all finished" if it was not there. I kept ducking underwater to try and cut the life raft free, but the life raft, being buoyant, was stuck under the boat. I must have tried this a dozen times. You can imagine it, going up and down, trying to hold on to the life raft rope so it wouldn't get taken away and cutting these other ropes. And all the time the boat was getting swept around.

'Each time I had to immediately go back to my little bolt-hole so that I could warm up. I would have to stay there for about two hours to warm up, then go back down to have another go. The thing that terrified me, terrified me, was that I was in my little black hole, and I kept saying to meself, "I'm never going to make it."

'The only thing I had, really, was some chocolate, which was in my pocket because I couldn't keep it anywhere else. It was getting wet and salty and was not particularly nice. I had run out of water but I had a survival water maker, which is like a little jack for a car. It basically boiled down to a bit of chocolate and the water maker, that was it.

I would crawl up into my little corner and think. I kept thinking through the logistics of what was going on and try to work out the best way to utilise my opportunities.

'Then sometimes I'd hit a brick wall and say, "The opportunity is so small there is no opportunity". I can't sing and I didn't talk to myself, not really. The logistics (were) that I was coming to an end. It was really a question of working out the possibilities to make the end last as long as possible.

'I started asking myself, "Am I really preparing my grave?" I really believe I was just on the brink. I got to the point where I was thinking in hours. Most of the time I was thinking logically. There were one or two times when I was fading off into bad situations but then you had to pull yourself back together again.

'I think if I was picking words to describe it, it would be a miracle. An absolute miracle.'

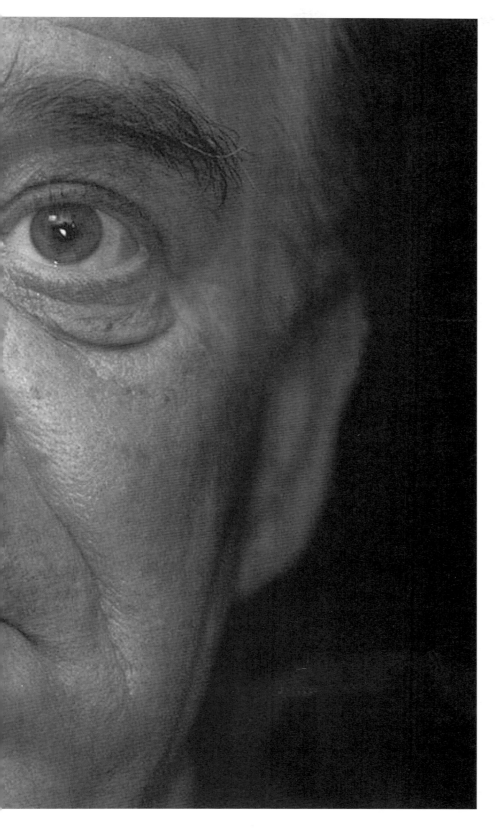

Imagine being shut
in a small, pitch-black
closet. You are freezing,
wet and the closet is
rocking wildly. This
man lived through it
for 89 hours.

Call of the Wild

'People walk to the South Pole, they go down to the sea, they go up as high as they can, they go sideways, whatever. If all these things were taken away it would be a bit like the taming of mankind.'

What is it that drives people to pursue daredevil adventures in order to prove their worth? To walk that fine line between life and death in order to explore uncharted lands, sail the roughest seas or scale the highest peaks?

Tony Bullimore, Raphael Dinelli, Thierry Dubois, Peter Hillary, Tim Macartney-Snape and Isabelle Autissier put their lives at risk every time they pit themselves against the elements in the name of adventure and adrenalin.

Are they heroic, irresponsible, mad, or extraordinary?

Certainly the advance of technology has pushed adventurers to ever greater challenges. And technology played a hand in the successful rescue of Tony Bullimore, Thierry Dubois and Raphael Dinelli in January 1997 after their yachts capsized in the Southern Ocean during the Vendee Globe race. As veteran Australian sailor David Adams puts it, ten or even five years ago, 'these guys would have been dead. You wouldn't have known about it.' Satellite communication helped to narrow down the search area and ensured a faster rate of response on the part of rescuers.

Yet technology alone does not explain the capacity of those caught in strife to set their minds on staying alive. Peter Hillary, who followed his father Edmund to the top of the world, says that the best equipment plays only a minor role in what drives the adventurer to extra heights. 'The rest lies with you: do you have the drive, the psyche, the power?'

In order to keep hope and body going, each adventurer has to draw on his or her psychological and physical resources. Bullimore describes his survival as coming from 'sheer determination . . . hanging on in there and believing something would happen, and just keep fighting'.

It is the contemplation of success, not the fear of failure, that drives these risk-takers. They have a high level of practical ability, are experienced and know what they are getting themselves into. John Taske, who was part of an expedition to Mount Everest, says, 'I never think I am going to die . . . Every one of us, including the sailors who know their job very well, have in their own minds empirically a level of risk which they are prepared to take. Now it may appear to non-sailors and non-mountaineers that the risk is inordinately high. But because you are confident in your abilities, the risk that I see is not that high.'

Of course, the impulse to fight for life is not confined to those we call adventurers. Instances of otherwise ordinary people displaying courage to survive experiences made extreme by the severe elements, the distance from rescue, or both, are legion.

Melbourne psychiatrist Tim Watson-Munro thinks people have peak and flow experiences that impel some to take risks out of a 'greater sense of exhilaration, and overwhelming sense of oneness with the universe. These individuals tend to feel this more deeply than those of us who stay at home.'

Tim Macartney-Snape, the first Australian to climb Mount Everest, believes that the spirit of adventure is innate, just closer to the surface in some people. 'Extreme situations of survival put your senses at a peak. You really have to take notice of everything around you. You become almost super-aware and that intensity lives on afterwards . . . And it is addictive, once you experience something like that.'

Is that why these adventurers keep going back to the mountain or ocean that nearly killed them?

Watson-Munro sees them as 'adrenalin junkies'. For them, 'The sense of danger and achievement outweigh the fear of losing their lives.'

The actions of adventurers reaffirm the ecstacy of being alive.

Bullimore believes it is part of the human condition to push forward the boundaries of endeavour: 'People walk to the South Pole, they go down to the sea, they go up as high as they can, they go sideways, whatever. If all these things were taken away it would be a bit like the taming of mankind.'

The actions of these adventurers reaffirm the ecstasy of being alive, and further strengthen their urge to explore and understand the world – something those among us less content to answer the call of the wild can only hope to experience vicariously.

Safe aboard HMAS Adelaide

'It's people like you who've made my luck' – Tony Bullimore and his rescuers.

'It's all in a day's work.'

'I'm starting to believe in miracles,' said HMAS *Adelaide's* skipper, Captain Raydon Gates, as an RAAF Orion, which had helped coordinate the rescues, roared past about 30 metres above the waves, its slipstream visible in the grey haze.

'It was a team job. You all make me very proud,' the skipper said.

Just four hours after the French yachtsman Thierry Dubois walked out of the Seahawk helicopter that had winched him out of his lifeboat, the injured Tony Bullimore was lying on the floor of a rescue boat.

Despite frostbitten feet, Bullimore was ecstatic to be standing on deck. After an hour of treatment in the frigate's sick bay he was keen to tell of his experiences: 'I don't mind telling the world, I've become more human. In these last six days I'm a different person.

'I'm feeling much better, it's like a step forward back to sanity,' said Bullimore. 'It's really a case of

tremendous support from the RAAF and the RAN that has helped tremendously.'

Staggering back on frostbitten feet, he encountered a sailor who had been supplying the captain with tea. 'Would you like a drink?' she asked.

'I wouldn't mind, if it's not too much trouble,' said Bullimore. 'I don't want to be a nuisance.'

'You're a very lucky man,' she said.

'No, no,' he demurred. 'It's people like you who've made my luck.'

It took only moments for the compliment to be relayed throughout the ship.

Morale on board the frigate was high as congratulatory faxes flooded in from around the world. The crew was even organising a T-shirt design to commemorate the event. 'It's all in a day's work for us but the crew have done a great job and deserve recognition,' Captain Raydon Gates said.

Looking at life: Tony Bullimore thanks Chief Petty Officer Peter Wicker, who pulled him from the Southern Ocean.

Brothers in arms: Thierry Dubois greets fellow solo yachtsman Tony Bullimore aboard HMAS Adelaide.

Once aboard HMAS Adelaide, Tony Bullimore told Chief Petty Officer Peter Wicker: 'If you didn't have a beard I'd kiss you.' Bullimore's composure immediately endeared himself to his rescuers

To life! Thierry Dubois and Tony Bullimore celebrate with their RAN rescuers.

The rescuers and the rescued: the men and women involved in the rescue with Tony Bullimore and Thierry Dubois.

Rescued yachtsmen Dubois and Bullimore listen to a service delivered HMAS Adelaide's chaplain, Barrie Yesberg, on the flight deck.

Giving thanks

About fifty men and women took part in a flight deck service of thanksgiving for the successful rescues in the Southern Ocean. The service was led by HMAS *Adelaide's* chaplain, Barrie Yesberg, and attended by Tony Bullimore and Thierry Dubois.

'Their very presence here with us is miraculous,' said Chaplain Barrie Yesberg. 'Thanks for being part of their lives and giving life back to them,' he told the congregation.

After the 30-minute service, Bullimore said he had scuttled navy public relations plans for him to be pushed down the frigate's gangway in a wheelchair at tomorrow's welcoming ceremony in Fremantle.

Captain Raydon Gates said the crew had become quite attached to the rescued yachtsmen and that the berthing of the frigate would mark a sad moment for them.

Dubois and Bullimore had been living in the Petty Officer's quarters and had dined in the Chief Petty Officer's mess. The pair were to join officers tonight to celebrate their last dinner together.

Bullimore had only praise for the men and women behind his rescue: 'It's been fantastic, in the first instance with the coordination of the rescue, the professionalism, the training and the sheer determination to help us.'

Bullimore disembarking HMAS Adelaide in Fremantle.

Sitting pat: Tony Bullimore and his fellow survivor, Thierry Dubois, on arrival at Fremantle.

On solid ground again:
Dubois's face says it all.

Reflecting on life: Thierry Dubois (left) and RAAF Orion pilot Flight Lieutenant Ludo Dierickx, who first spotted Dubois in the Southern Ocean, at the Edinburgh RAAF base in South Australia.

A dock welcome fit for heroes

'I've been given another chance and it's through the efforts of Australia.'

An estimated 6000 people gathered at Fremantle today to give a hero's welcome to HMAS *Adelaide* and the two round-the-world yachtsmen saved from the Southern Ocean, Thierry Dubois and Tony Bullimore. More than 40 dignitaries were among the guests, including federal and state politicians and the high commissioners of Britain and France. About 80 journalists from Europe and Australia were also present. The event was telecast live around the world.

Frenchman Thierry Dubois hopes to be reunited with his mother, Bridgette Dubois, and his girlfriend Murielle Dehoue, 28, who are now in Fremantle. Englishman Tony Bullimore will meet his wife of 35 years, Lalel, later in the morning when she arrives from Britain.

Speaking in French, Dubois said he was 'amazed at the welcome and amazed at how Australians respect life'.

'We are not the heroes,' he said. 'It is the seamen who have the spirit of help. Thank you to all these guys.'

Bullimore handled the several thousand well-wishers, a welcoming party of politicians and about a hundred journalists from around the world with style and spirit. The man who still wants to sail solo around the world – if he can get a sponsor – told the cheering people that both he and Dubois owed their lives to the professionalism and dedication of the Australian Defence Force.

At one stage he turned from the dignitaries, microphones and media on the wharf. He gestured at the grey bulk of his rescue vessel behind him, the 4000-tonne guided-missile frigate HMAS *Adelaide*, with most of its 140 sailors lining the deck, and said: 'If it wasn't for the defence forces and this great ship here, and every man and woman who sails on this ship, the professionalism and dedication, the inbuilt spirit of Australia, I'm positive, I'm absolutely no doubt at all positive, I wouldn't be here now.

'I've been given another chance and it's through the efforts of Australia.'

Around 6000 people gathered to welcome Thierry Dubois and Tony Bullimore back to land. Both survivors said they owed their lives to the professionalism and dedication of all those involved in the rescue operation, and to the spirit of Australia.

He's alive!

Lalel Bullimore reflecting on her husband's rescue: 'The relief was truly wonderful.'

Tony Bullimore's survival was heralded at his home in Bristol, England, by the simultaneous ringing of half-a-dozen telephones. 'The old dog is alive, he's bloody alive,' Lalel Bullimore shouted with joy.

Boat builders, friends and family members had gathered in the house in Westbury Park to wait with Lalel, Bullimore's wife. The couple have no children.

Upon hearing her husband was alive, Lalel disappeared beneath hugs and embraces. People were shouting and cheering all over the house. Bottles of champagne were produced and corks popped.

'The relief was truly wonderful,' Lalel Bullimore said. 'We hugged and kissed, we jumped up and down, opened champagne and ran out into the street shouting "He's alive!"'

Emotion and colour in Fremantle at the welcome of the rescued yachtsmen and the rescue crew aboard HMAS Adelaide.

The dramatic rescues of Raphael Dinelli, Thierry Dubois and Tony Bullimore prompted a flood of international praise.

The Queen asked the Governor-General, Sir William Deane, to pass on her congratulations to the crews and Bullimore: 'I would be grateful if you would pass on both my congratulations to all members of the Australian defence forces who have made possible the two dramatic rescues in the Southern Ocean over these recent days,' she said. 'And through HMAS *Adelaide*, my warm good wishes to Tony Bullimore on his extraordinary feat of survival.'

Sir William applauded all those involved, saying the nation was 'very proud of this wonderful demonstration of the ability, efficiency, resourcefulness and bravery of its service men and women'.

Britain's Prime Minister, John Major, said: 'It is a tribute to [the rescue team's] skill and seamanship – as well as Mr Bullimore's resilience – that they succeeded in finding and recovering him in such appalling conditions so far offshore.'

Phillipe Jeantot was overjoyed by the dramatic rescues. 'We want very much to congratulate all the people who have been involved . . . they have proven their knowledge, their seamanship and their willing service to sailors.'

In letters sent to Captain Raydon Gates, commander of HMAS *Adelaide* and Wing Commander Ian Pearson, the Prime Minister, John Howard, said that 'people around the world watched your efforts and hoped the two sailors could be brought back to safety. You and your rescue team delivered an outcome many believed was not possible considering the dangerous circumstances in which you carried out your work.

'Australians are proud of the way you have conducted yourselves with complete professionalism, and your efforts in Antarctic conditions merit our unreserved admiration.'

Queen leads praise for rescue crews

'A tribute to their skill and seamanship.'

Messages of congratulations and thanks to the Australian Defence Force from Queen Elizabeth, Governor General Sir William Deane, Australian Prime Minister John Howard, and British Prime Minister John Major.

A toast to a job well done: Dubois and members of the RAAF pay tribute to the skill and professionalism of the rescue team.

A sea fit for heroes

'Keep going, never give up. Keep going, keep going. You'll win through in the end if you keep going.' – Tony Bullimore

The significance of the oceans that cover five-sevenths of the world can hardly be overestimated, and is recorded in religion ('and the spirit of God moved upon the face of the waters') and the poetic imagination (from 'The Rime of the Ancient Mariner' to 'The Wreck of the Hesperus').

There are, of course, those who query the expense entailed when solo mariners are lost or in peril and rescue parties are sent out after them. Certainly the race organisers should strive for improved safety, consider insurance schemes, the pros and cons of having a well-equipped mother ship accompany future race competitors, and other relevant strategies to ensure the wellbeing of the competitors. But perhaps we all need to be reminded sometimes that life often asks of us endurance and courage, skill and planning: qualities that those of us who lead comparatively mundane existences need to draw on to survive.

The bravery of those rescued and of their rescuers at the Australian Maritime Safety Authority and in the Defence Force has revived the true meaning of the word 'success'. Inspiration cannot be measured, but it is real, and the exceptional few who sacrifice greatly to live out their dreams are the stuff of heroes. Shortly after his dramatic rescue Bullimore received three firm offers to make a film of his ordeal and already an Australian author is ghosting Bullimore's story, to be released later in 1997.

The refusal to lose hope amid the most terrifying of circumstances – Tony Bullimore spent four days huddled under the hull of his upturned yacht *Global Exide Challenger* – has inspired a world with hope, and given us all something extra.

Acknowledgements

Coordination

Martin Daly and Sally Dugan of *The Age*, Melbourne.
Special thanks to David Jeffcoat of Defence Public Relations.

Text

Martin Daly, Andrew Darby, David Elias, Duncan Graham and Ben Mitchell of
The Age, Melbourne; Kevan Wolfe of *The Sunday Age*, Melbourne; Brian Woodley
and Belinda Hickman of *The Australian*.

Graphics

Jamie Browne, Sarah Cook and Monique Westermann of *The Age*, Melbourne;
Edi Sizgoric of the *Sydney Morning Herald*, Sydney.

Photographs

Kerry Berrington, *Sunday Times*, Perth – pages 2, 59, 64, 77 (inset).
Sport the Library – pages 8, 10, 35, 50, 52.
Bruce Miller – pages 9 (right), 21 (insets).
Department of Defence – pages 12, 17 (top), 28 (insets), 30, 32, 34, 41, 62.
    RAN Photographic
    LSPH Steve Gurnett, Navy Photographic Unit
    PO Kym Degener, Navy Photographic Unit
    92 Wing Photographers, RAAF Base, Edinburgh, South Australia
Guy Magowan, West Australian Newspapers – pages 14, 40, 54, 57, 83 (inset), 90, 94.
F.Bouchon, AP – page 16.
Tony McDonough, *The Age* – pages 17 (bottom), 18, 46, 64 (inset), 72, 76, 77, 78, 81,
  86 (inset), 88.
Mark Baker, Reuters – pages 20, 71.
Andrew de la Rue, *The Age* – page 21.
Annaliese Frank, *The Age* – pages 22, 28, 29, 82.
Tony Ashby, West Australian Newspapers – page 26.
Greg Woods, Agence France Presse – pages 36, 37, 38.
F. Mousis, Reuters – pages 42, 48.
Bill Hatto, West Australian Newspapers – pages 58, 60, 80.
David Gray, Reuters – page 84.
Jason South, *The Age* – pages 86, 92.
Peter Batchelor, AP – page 91(right).
AP/ANDIA – page 95.